Basic Computation Series

Working with Perimeter and Area

Loretta M. Taylor, Ed. D.

Harold D. Taylor, Ed. D.

Dale Seymour Publications®
Parsippany, New Jersey

Executive Editor: Catherine Anderson
Editorial Manager: John Nelson
Development Editor: Deborah J. Slade
Production/Manufacturing Director: Janet Yearian
Sr. Production/Manufacturing Coordinator: Roxanne Knoll
Design Director: Jim O'Shea
Design Manager: Jeff Kelly
Cover Designer: Monika Popowitz
Interior Designer: Christy Butterfield
Composition: Joe Conte

Copyright © 2000 by Dale Seymour Publications.

All rights reserved. Printed in the United States of America.

This book is published by Dale Seymour Publications®, an imprint of Pearson Learning.

Dale Seymour Publications
299 Jefferson Road
Parsippany, NJ 07054-0480
Customer Service: 800-872-1100

Limited Reproduction Permission: The authors and publisher hereby grant permission to the teacher who purchases this book, or the teacher for whom the book is purchased, to reproduce up to 100 copies of any part of this book for use with his or her students. Any further duplication is prohibited.

ISBN 0-7690-0120-3
Order Number DS21922

2 3 4 5 6 7 8 9 10-ML-03 02 01

Authors of the Basic Computation Series 2000

Loretta M. Taylor is a retired high school mathematics teacher. During her teaching career, she taught at Hillsdale High School in San Mateo, California; Crestmoor High School in San Bruno, California; Patterson High School in Patterson, California; Round Valley Union High School in Covelo, California; and Farmington High School in Farmington, New Mexico. Dr. Taylor obtained a B.S. in mathematics from Southeastern Oklahoma State University, and both an M.A. in mathematics and an Ed.D. in mathematics education from the University of Northern Colorado. She has been active in professional organizations at the local, state, and national levels, including the National Council of Teachers of Mathematics, the California Mathematics Council, the National Education Association, and the California Teachers Association. She has given a variety of talks and workshops at numerous conferences, schools, and universities. Dr. Taylor is a member of Lambda Sigma Tau, a national honorary science fraternity, and is coauthor of *Paper and Scissors Polygons and More, Algebra Book 1, Algebra Book 2,* and *Developing Skills in Algebra 1.* In retirement, she continues to be an active mathematics author and is involved with community organizations.

Harold D. Taylor is a retired high school mathematics teacher, having taught at Aragon High School in San Mateo, California; as well as at Patterson High School in Patterson, California; Round Valley Union High School in Covelo, California; and Farmington High School in Farmington, New Mexico. He has served in high schools not only as a mathematics teacher, but also as a mathematics department head and as an assistant principal. He received a B.S. in mathematics from Southeastern Oklahoma State University, and both an M.A. in mathematics and an Ed.D. in mathematics education from the University of Northern Colorado. Dr. Taylor has been very active in a number of professional organizations, having worked in a variety of significant capacities for the National Council of Teachers of Mathematics and the California Mathematics Council. He was chairman of the Publicity and Information Committee and the Local Organizing Committee for the Fourth International Congress on Mathematics Education at Berkeley, California, was on the writing team of the California Assessment Test, and was a member of the California State Mathematics Framework and Criteria Committee, chairing the California State Mathematics Framework Addendum Committee. Since 1966, he has spoken at more than one hundred local, state, and national meetings on mathematics and mathematics education. Dr. Taylor is author of *Ten Mathematics Projects and Career Education Infusion,* and coauthor of *Algebra Book 1, Algebra Book 2,* and *Developing Skills in Algebra 1.* In 1989 he was the California recipient of the Presidential Award for Excellence in Teaching Secondary Mathematics. In retirement, Dr. Taylor is continuing to produce mathematics materials for the classroom, and also serves his community as County Judge in Custer County, Colorado, having been appointed to this position by Governor Roy Romer.

Table of Contents

A Note of Introduction — iv
About the Program — v
Student Record Sheet — ix

Section 1 Perimeter and Area of Rectangles — **1**

Finding Length, Width, Perimeter, and Area — 4, 5, 6, 7, 8, 9, 10, 11, 12, 13
Drawing Rectangles with Given Area or Perimeter — 14, 16, 18, 20, 22
Drawing Rectangles with Given Area and Perimeter — 15, 17, 19, 21, 23

Section 2 Perimeter and Area of Rectangles - English and Metric Units — **25**

Perimeter and Area of Rectangles – English Units — 27, 29, 31, 33, 35
Perimeter and Area of Rectangles – Metric Units — 28, 30, 32, 34, 36
Working with Perimeter and Area Formulas – English Units — 37, 39, 41, 43, 45
Working with Perimeter and Area Formulas – Metric Units — 38, 40, 42, 44, 46

Section 3 Perimeter and Area of Triangles, Parallelograms, and Trapezoids — **47**

Area of Right Triangles — 51, 53, 55, 57, 59
Drawing Right Triangles with Given Area — 52, 54, 56, 58, 60
Perimeter and Area of Right Triangles – English Units — 61, 63, 65, 67, 69
Perimeter and Area of Right Triangles – Metric Units — 62, 64, 66, 68, 70
Area of Triangles — 71, 73, 75, 77, 79
Drawing Triangles with Given Dimensions or Area — 72, 74, 76, 78, 80
Area and Perimeter of Triangles and Parallelograms — 81, 83, 85, 87, 89
Area and Perimeter of Trapezoids — 82, 84, 86, 88, 90

Answers to Exercises — **91**

Graph Paper — **94**

A Note of Introduction

To the Teacher
Some students are familiar with computational work but have never really mastered it. Perhaps this is a result of a lack of practice. With the *Basic Computation Series 2000*, you can provide students with as much practice as they need. You can teach, check up, reteach, and reinforce. You can give classwork and homework. If you wish, you can create a full year's course in basic computation, or you can provide skills maintenance when it's needed. All the work is here. Select the pages you want to use for the students who need them.

To the Student
You can't play a guitar before you learn the chords. You can't shoot a hook shot before you learn the lay-up. You can't pass a mathematics exam before you learn to compute, and you can't master computational skills until you learn the mathematical facts and procedures. Learning takes practice; there are no shortcuts. The pages in this book are for practice. Do your math every day and think about what you're doing. If you don't understand something, ask questions. Don't do too much work in your head; it's worth an extra sheet of paper to write down your steps. Also, be patient with yourself. Learning takes time.

Although calculators and other computational devices are readily available to most everyone, you will be forever handicapped if you are not able to perform basic mathematical computations without the aid of a mechanical or electronic computational device. Learn and master the procedures so that you can rely on your own abilities.

To the Parent
The importance of the development of mathematical skills cannot be emphasized enough. Mathematics is needed to estimate materials for a construction job or to price a car. It's needed to predict earthquakes and to prescribe medicine. It helps you determine how to stretch your dollars and pay your bills. This program provides the practice students need to develop the essential computational skills. Conventional algorithms are utilized throughout the *Basic Computation Series 2000*. You can help your children learn these skills. Give them your support and encouragement. Urge them to do their homework. Be there to answer their questions. Give them a quiet place to work. Make them feel good about trying. Your help can make the difference.

About the Program

What is the Basic Computation Series 2000?

The books in the *Basic Computation Series 2000* provide comprehensive practice on all the essential computational skills. There are nine practice books and a test book. The practice books consist of carefully sequenced drill worksheets organized in groups of five. The test book contains daily quizzes (160 quizzes in all), semester tests, and year-end tests written in standardized-test format.

Book 1	Working with Whole Numbers
Book 2	Understanding Fractions
Book 3	Working with Fractions
Book 4	Working with Decimals
Book 5	Working with Percents
Book 6	Understanding Measurement
Book 7	Working with Perimeter and Area
Book 8	Working with Surface Area and Volume
Book 9	Applying Computational Skills
Test Book 10	Basic Computation Quizzes and Tests

Who can use the Basic Computation Series 2000?

The *Basic Computation Series 2000* is appropriate for use by any person, young or old, who has not achieved computational proficiency. It may be used with any program calling for carefully sequenced computational practice. The material is especially suitable for use with students in fifth grade, middle school, junior high school, special education classes, and high school. It may be used by classroom teachers, substitute teachers, tutors, and parents. It is also useful for those in adult education, for those preparing for the General Education Development Test (GED), and for others wishing to study on their own.

What is in this book?

This book is a practice book. In addition to explanation and examples for the student, parent, and teacher, it contains student worksheets, answers, and a record sheet.

Worksheets

The worksheets are designed to give even the slowest student a chance to master the essential computational skills. Most worksheets come in five equivalent forms allowing for pretesting, practice, and post-testing on any particular skill. Each set of worksheets provides practice on only one or two specific skills, and the work progresses in very small steps from one set to the next. Instructions are clear and simple. Ample practice is provided on each page, giving students the opportunity to strengthen their skills. Answers to each problem are included in the back of the book.

Explanatory Material

The beginning of each section includes explanatory material designed to help students, parents, and teachers understand the material in the section and its purpose. Fully-worked examples show how to work each type of exercise. The example solutions are written in a straightforward manner so as to be easily understood.

Student Record Sheet

A record sheet is provided to help in recording progress and assessing instructional needs.

Answers

Answers to all problems are included in the back of the book.

How can the Basic Computation Series 2000 be used?

The materials in the *Basic Computation Series 2000* can serve as the major skeleton of a skills program or as supplements to any other computational skills program. The large number of worksheets provides a wide variety from which to choose and allows flexibility in structuring a program to meet individual needs. The following suggestions are offered to show how the *Basic Computation Series 2000* may be adapted to a particular situation.

Minimal Competency Practice

In various fields and schools, standardized tests are used for entrance, passage from one level to another, and certification of competency or proficiency prior to graduation. The materials in the *Basic Computation Series 2000* are particularly well-suited to preparing for any of the various mathematics competency tests, including the mathematics portion of the General Education Development Test (GED) used to certify high school equivalency.

Together, the books in the *Basic Computation Series 2000* provide practice on all the essential computational skills measured on competency tests. The semester tests and year-end tests from the test book are written in standardized-test format. These tests can be used as sample minimal competency tests. The worksheets can be used to brush up on skills measured by the competency tests.

Skills Maintenance

Since most worksheets come in five equivalent forms, the work can be organized into weekly units as suggested by the following schedule: A five-day schedule can begin on any day of the week. The authors' ideal schedule begins on Thursday, with pretesting and introduction of a skill, and follows with reteaching on Friday. Monday and Tuesday are for practice, touch-up teaching, reinforcing, and individualized instruction. Wednesday is test day. Daily quizzes from the *Basic Computation Series 2000 Quizzes And Tests Book* can be used on the drill-and-practice days for maintenance of previously-learned skills or diagnosis of skill deficiencies. Ideally, except for test days, a quiz may be given during the first fifteen minutes of a class period with the remainder of the period used for instruction and practice with other materials.

Authors' Suggested Teaching Schedule

	Day 1	Day 2	Day 3	Day 4	Day 5
Week 1	Pages 4 and 5 Pages 14 and 15	Pages 6 and 7 Pages 16 and 17	Pages 8 and 9 Paes 18 and 19	Pages 10 and 11 Pages 20 and 21	Pages 12 and 13 Pages 22 and 23
Week 2	Pages 27 and 28 Pages 37 and 38	Pages 29 and 30 Pages 39 and 40	Pages 31 and 32 Pages 41 and 42	Pages 33 and 34 Pages 43 and 44	Pages 35 and 36 Pages 45 and 46
Week 3	Pages 51 and 52 Pages 61 and 62	Pages 53 and 54 Pages 63 and 64	Pages 55 and 56 Pages 65 and 66	Pages 57 and 58 Pages 67 and 68	Pages 59 and 60 Pages 69 and 70
Week 4	Pages 71 and 72 Pages 81 and 82	Pages 73 and 74 Pages 83 and 84	Pages 75 and 76 Pages 85 and 86	Pages 77 and 78 Pages 87 and 88	Pages 79 and 80 Pages 89 and 90

Supplementary Drill

There are more than 18,000 problems in the *Basic Computation Series 2000*. When students need more practice with a given skill, use the appropriate worksheets from the series. They are suitable for classwork or homework practice following the teaching of a specific skill. With five equivalent pages for most worksheets, adequate practice is provided for each essential skill.

How are the materials prepared?

The books are designed with pages that can be easily reproduced. Permanent transparencies can be produced using a copy machine and special transparencies designed for this purpose. The program will run more smoothly if the student's work is stored in folders. Record sheets can be attached to the folders so that students, teachers, or parents can keep records of an individual's progress. Materials stored in this way are readily available for conferences with the student or parent.

Student Record Sheet

Worksheets Completed

Page Number

4	6	8	10
5	7	9	11

14	16	18	20
15	17	19	21

27	29	31	33
28	30	32	34

37	39	41	43
38	40	42	43

51	53	55	57
52	54	56	58

61	63	65	67
62	64	66	68

71	73	75	77
72	74	76	78

81	83	85	87
82	84	86	88

12
13
22
23
35
36
45
46
59
60
69
70
79
80
89
90

Quiz Grades

No.	Score

Checklist

Skill Mastered	Date
❏ finding length, width, perimeter, and area of rectangles	_____
❏ drawing rectangles with given area and/or perimeter	_____
❏ finding perimeter and area of rectangles using English units	_____
❏ finding perimeter and area of rectangles using metric units	_____
❏ finding area of right triangles	_____
❏ drawing right triangles with given area	_____
❏ finding perimeter and area of right triangles using English units	_____
❏ finding perimeter and area of right triangles using metric units	_____
❏ finding area of triangles	_____
❏ drawing triangles with given dimensions or area	_____
❏ finding area and perimeter of triangles and parallelograms	_____
❏ finding area and perimeter of trapezoids	_____

Notes
_____
_____
_____
_____

Perimeter and Area of Rectangles

SECTION 1

The perimeter of a geometric figure is the distance around the figure. Perimeter can be measured in either English or metric units, or, as in some of the exercises in this book, simply in "units," a non-specific type of measurement. Perimeter is a linear measurement, as it indicates distance.

A rectangle is a shape like the page of a book. It has four sides and four angles. Opposite sides are both parallel and equal in length, and each angle is a right angle. The dimensions of a rectangle are called its *length* and *width*. In general, it does not matter which dimension is considered the length and which is considered width. The length is usually represented by the letter "l," and the width by the letter "w."

Example 1: Find the length, width, and perimeter of the rectangle.

Solution: The number of squares on the side marked l is 5; thus, the length is 5 units.
The number of squares on the side marked w is 4; thus, the width is 4 units.
The perimeter is the distance around the rectangle, which is 5 + 4 + 5 + 4, or 18 units.

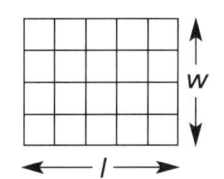

The area of a rectangle is the number of square units in the interior of the rectangle. It is measured in square units rather than linear units. A square inch is a square that measures one inch on each side. A square centimeter is a square that measures one centimeter on each side. Unit squares, which are used in some examples, are squares that measure one unit on each side.

Example 2: Find the area of the rectangle in Example 1.

Solution: There are 20 squares within the rectangle; thus, the area is 20 square units.

Formulas may be used as shortcuts for finding the perimeter and area of geometric figures. Formulas for finding the perimeter, P, and the area, A, of a rectangle are as follows:

$$P = 2l + 2w$$
$$A = l \times w$$

(Note: In the perimeter formula, "$2l$" and "$2w$" represent two times the length and two times the width, respectively. When two values are written without an operation symbol between them, the implied operation is multiplication. Implied multiplication is used in many mathematical formulas.)

Basic Computation Series 2000: Working with Perimeter and Area
SECTION 1 Perimeter and Area of Rectangles

Example 3: Use formulas to find the perimeter and area of the rectangle.

Solution: The length of the rectangle is 6 units and the width is 5 units.

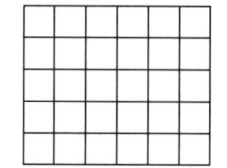

$$P = 2l + 2w$$
$$P = 2 \times 6 + 2 \times 5$$
$$P = 12 + 10$$
$$P = 22$$

Thus, the perimeter is 22 units.

$$A = l \times w$$
$$A = 6 \times 5$$
$$A = 30$$

Thus, the area is 30 square units.

Example 4: Use graph paper to draw 3 different-shaped rectangles, each with area 30 square units. State the number of units in the length, width, and perimeter of each rectangle. (Note: a blackline master for graph paper is provided on page 94.)

Solution: If the area of a rectangle must be 30 square units, the possible dimensions are:

$l = 30$ and $w = 1$
$l = 15$ and $w = 2$
$l = 10$ and $w = 3$
$l = 6$ and $w = 5$

There are no other possibilities (using whole numbers of units) since all the factors of 30 have been utilized. Three possible rectangles are shown below.

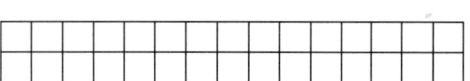

$l = 15$ units, $w = 2$ units
$P = 2 \times 15 + 2 \times 2$
$P = 34$ units

$l = 10$ units, $w = 3$ units
$P = 2 \times 10 + 2 \times 3$
$P = 26$ units

$l = 6$ units, $w = 5$ units
$P = 2 \times 6 + 2 \times 5$
$P = 22$ units

Example 5: Use graph paper to draw 3 different-shaped rectangles, each with perimeter 26 units. State the dimensions and area of each.

Solution: If the perimeter must be 26 units, the sum of the length and width must be 13 units. The possible dimensions (using only whole numbers) are:

$l = 12$ and $w = 1$
$l = 11$ and $w = 2$
$l = 10$ and $w = 3$
$l = 9$ and $w = 4$
$l = 8$ and $w = 5$
$l = 7$ and $w = 6$

Three possible rectangles are shown below.

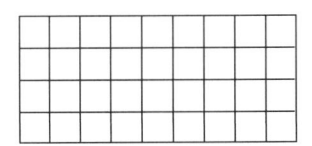

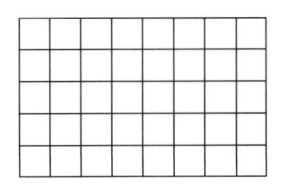

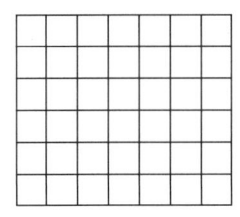

$l = 9$ units, $w = 4$ units
$A = 9 \times 4$
$A = 36$ square units

$l = 8$ units, $w = 5$ units
$A = 8 \times 5$
$A = 40$ square units

$l = 7$ units, $w = 6$ units
$A = 7 \times 6$
$A = 42$ square units

Example 6: Use graph paper to draw a rectangle with area 20 square units and perimeter 24 units.

Solution: A rectangle whose area is 20 square units must have one of the following pairs of dimensions:

$l = 20$ and $w = 1$
$l = 10$ and $w = 2$
$l = 5$ and $w = 4$

Calculate the perimeter of each possible rectangle.

$l = 20, w = 1$
$P = 2 \times 20 + 2 \times 1$
$P = 42$ units

$l = 10, w = 2$
$P = 2 \times 10 + 2 \times 2$
$P = 24$ units

$l = 5, w = 4$
$P = 2 \times 5 + 2 \times 4$
$P = 18$ units

Therefore, the rectangle with area 20 square units and perimeter 24 units has length 10 units and width 2 units.

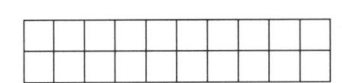

Basic Computation Series 2000: Working with Perimeter and Area
SECTION 1 Perimeter and Area of Rectangles

Finding Length, Width, Perimeter, and Area

For each rectangle, find the number of units in the length, the width, and the perimeter, and the number of square units in the area.

1. length = __10__
   width = __10__
   perimeter = __40__
   area = __100__

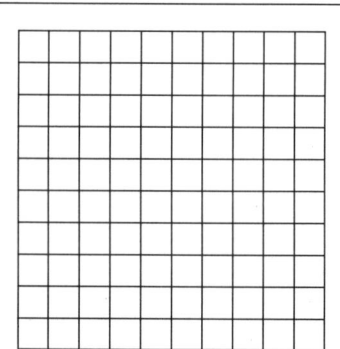

2. length = _____
   width = _____
   perimeter = _____
   area = _____

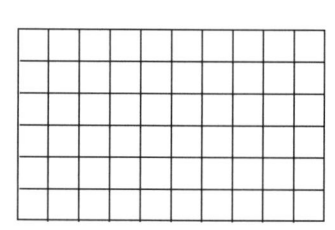

3. length = _____
   width = _____
   perimeter = _____
   area = _____

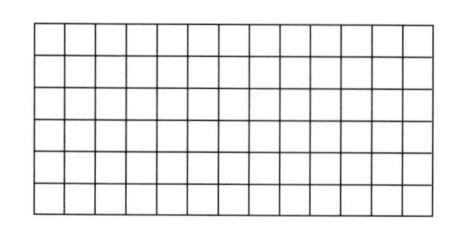

4. length = _____
   width = _____
   perimeter = _____
   area = _____

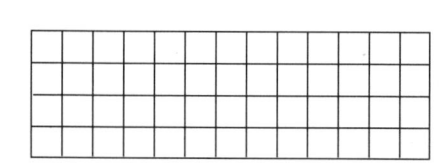

5. length = _____
   width = _____
   perimeter = _____
   area = _____

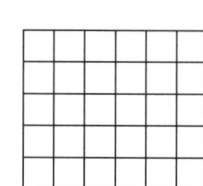

Basic Computation Series 2000: Working with Perimeter and Area

SECTION 1 Perimeter and Area of Rectangles

NAME _____   DATE _____

Finding Length, Width, Perimeter, and Area

For each rectangle, find the number of units in the length, the width, and the perimeter, and the number of square units in the area.

1. length = __9__
   width = __3__
   perimeter = __24__
   area = __27__

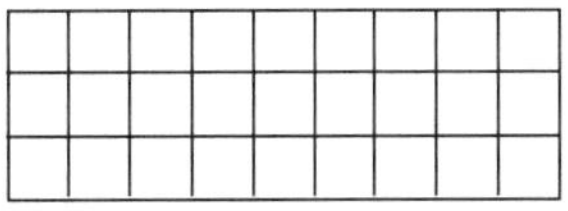

2. length = _____
   width = _____
   perimeter = _____
   area = _____

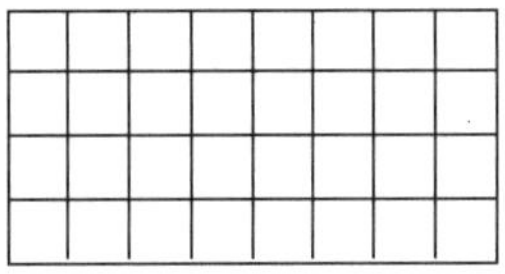

3. length = _____
   width = _____
   perimeter = _____
   area = _____

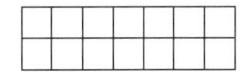

4. length = _____
   width = _____
   perimeter = _____
   area = _____

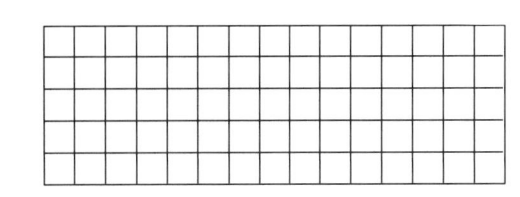

5. length = _____
   width = _____
   perimeter = _____
   area = _____

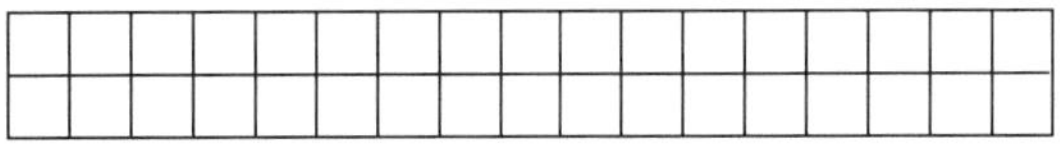

Basic Computation Series 2000: Finding Area and Perimeter
SECTION 1 Perimeter and Area of Rectangles

Finding Length, Width, Perimeter, and Area

For each rectangle, find the number of units in the length, the width, and the perimeter, and the number of square units in the area.

1. length = __15__
   width = __12__
   perimeter = __54__
   area = __180__

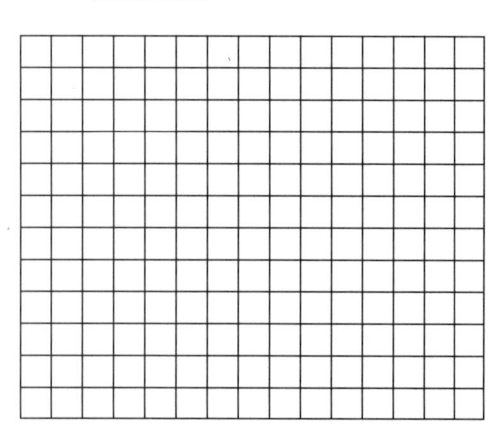

2. length = _____
   width = _____
   perimeter = _____
   area = _____

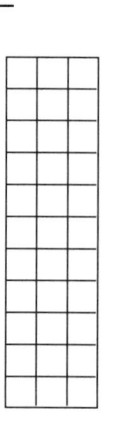

3. length = _____ width = _____ perimeter = _____ area = _____

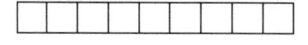

4. length = _____
   width = _____
   perimeter = _____
   area = _____

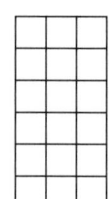

5. length = _____
   width = _____
   perimeter = _____
   area = _____

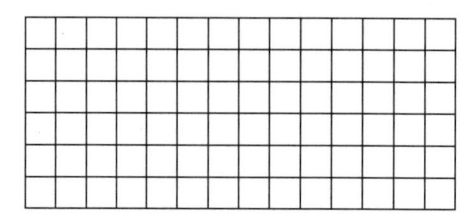

NAME _____   DATE _____

Finding Length, Width, Perimeter, and Area

For each rectangle, find the number of units in the length, the width, and the perimeter, and the number of square units in the area.

1. length = __6__

   width = __11__

   perimeter = __34__

   area = __66__

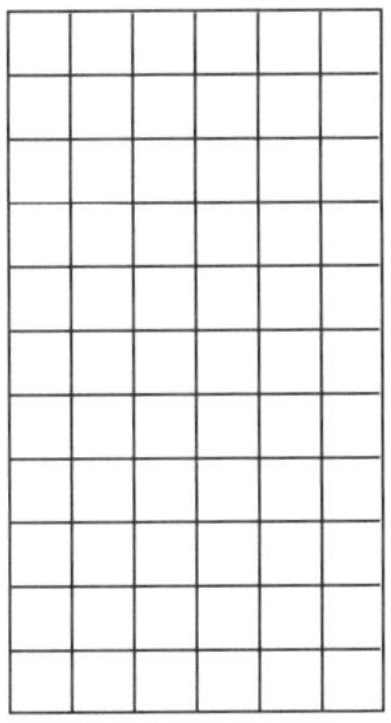

2. length = _____

   width = _____

   perimeter = _____

   area = _____

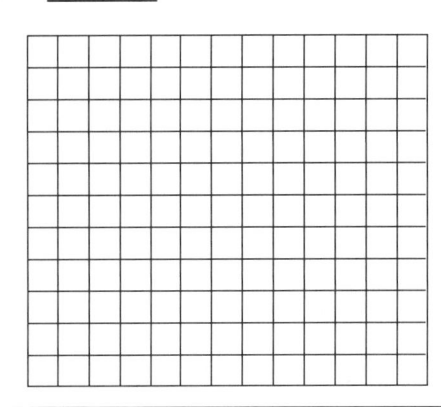

3. length = _____

   width = _____

   perimeter = _____

   area = _____

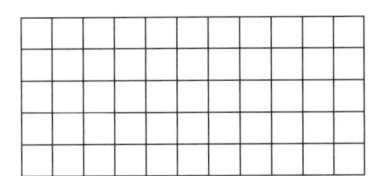

4. length = _____

   width = _____

   perimeter = _____

   area = _____

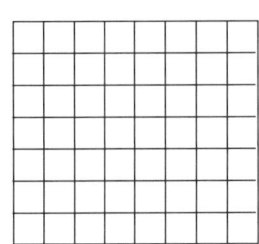

5. length = _____   width = _____   perimeter = _____   area = _____

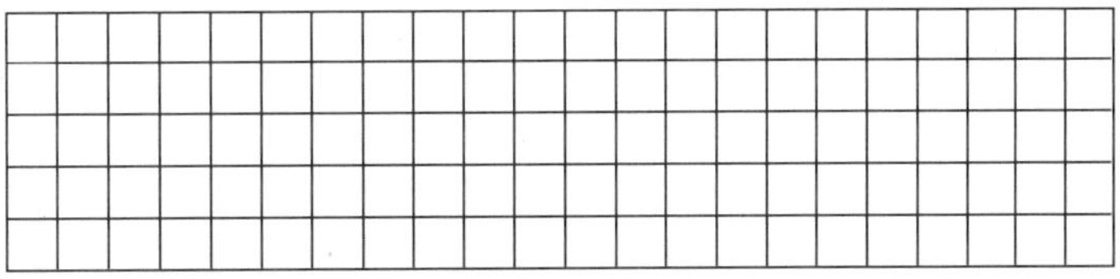

Basic Computation Series 2000: Working with Perimeter and Area
SECTION 1 Perimeter and Area of Rectangles

Finding Length, Width, Perimeter, and Area

For each rectangle, find the number of units in the length, the width, and the perimeter, and the number of square units in the area.

1. length = __12__
   width = __6__
   perimeter = __36__
   area = __72__

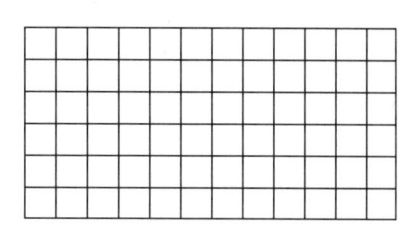

2. length = _____
   width = _____
   perimeter = _____
   area = _____

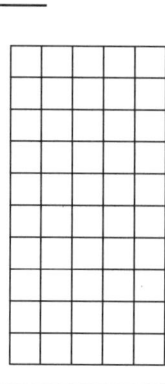

3. length = _____   width = _____   perimeter = _____   area = _____

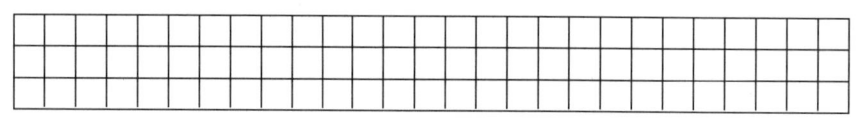

4. length = _____
   width = _____
   perimeter = _____
   area = _____

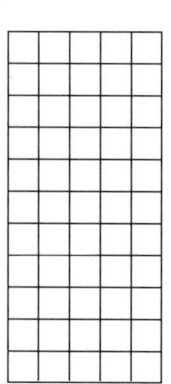

5. length = _____
   width = _____
   perimeter = _____
   area = _____

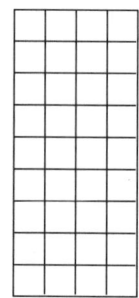

Basic Computation Series 2000: Working with Perimeter and Area

SECTION 1 Perimeter and Area of Rectangles

NAME _____   DATE _____

Finding Length, Width, Perimeter, and Area

For each rectangle, find the number of units in the length, the width, and the perimeter, and the number of square units in the area.

1. length = __6__
   width = __15__
   perimeter = __42__
   area = __90__

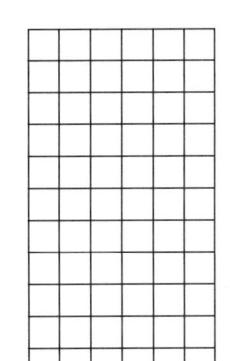

2. length = _____
   width = _____
   perimeter = _____
   area = _____

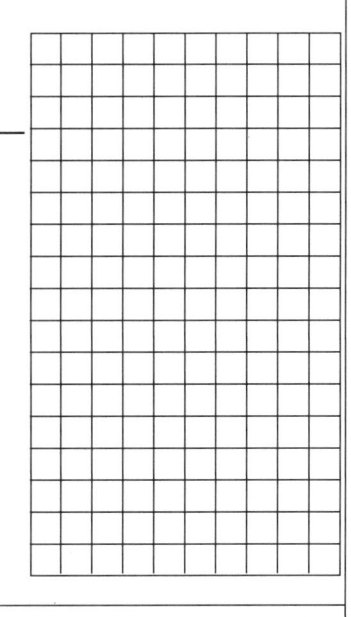

3. length = _____
   width = _____
   perimeter = _____
   area = _____

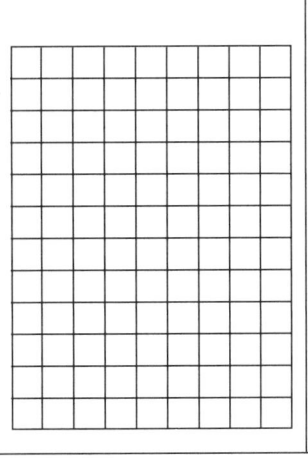

4. length = _____
   width = _____
   perimeter = _____
   area = _____

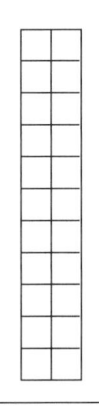

5. length = _____   width = _____   perimeter = _____   area = _____

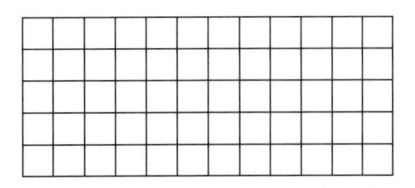

Basic Computation Series 2000: Working with Perimeter and Area
SECTION 1 Perimeter and Area of Rectangles

NAME _____ DATE _____

Finding Length, Width, Perimeter, and Area

For each rectangle, find the number of units in the length, the width, and the perimeter, and the number of square units in the area.

1. length = __11__
   width = __16__
   perimeter = __54__
   area = __176__

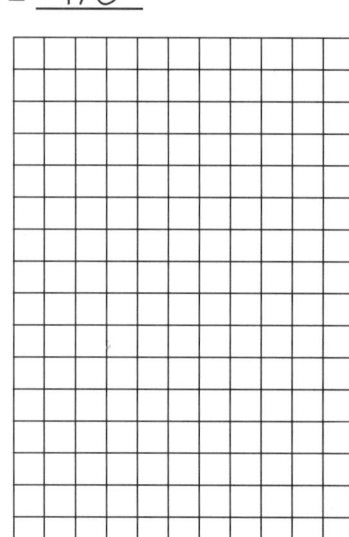

2. length = _____
   width = _____
   perimeter = _____
   area = _____

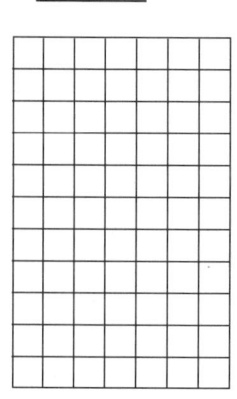

3. length = _____
   width = _____
   perimeter = _____
   area = _____

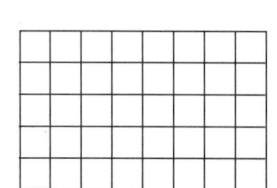

4. length = _____
   width = _____
   perimeter = _____
   area = _____

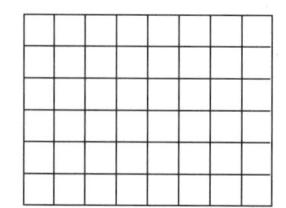

5. length = _____   width = _____   perimeter = _____   area = _____

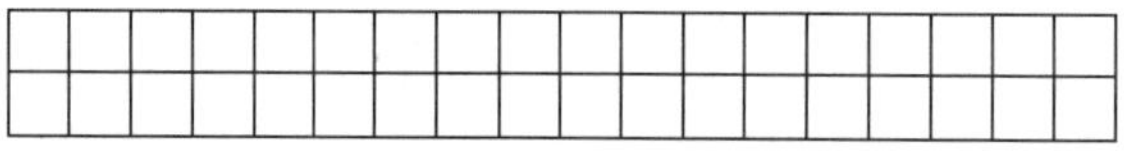

Basic Computation Series 2000: Working with Perimeter and Area
SECTION 1 Perimeter and Area of Rectangles

NAME   DATE

Finding Length, Width, Perimeter, and Area

For each rectangle, find the number of units in the length, the width, and the perimeter, and the number of square units in the area.

1. length = __7__
   width = __14__
   perimeter = __42__
   area = __98__

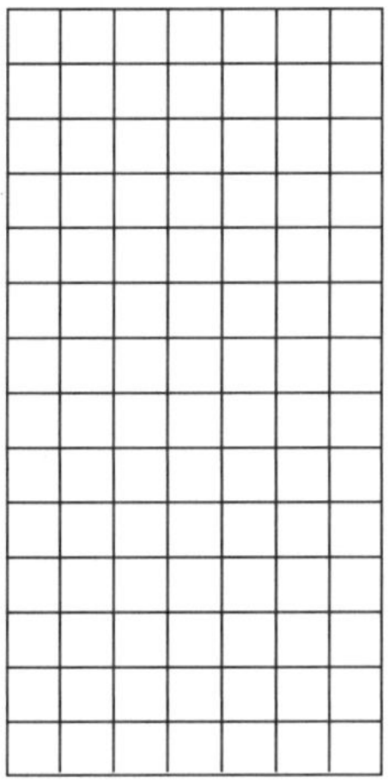

2. length = _____
   width = _____
   perimeter = _____
   area = _____

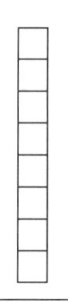

3. length = _____
   width = _____
   perimeter = _____
   area = _____

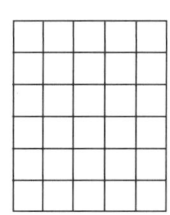

4. length = _____
   width = _____
   perimeter = _____
   area = _____

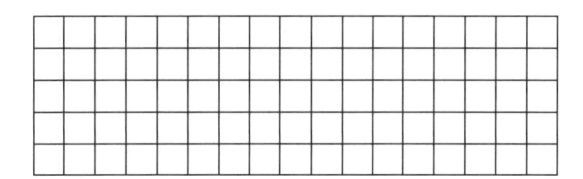

5. length = _____
   width = _____
   perimeter = _____
   area = _____

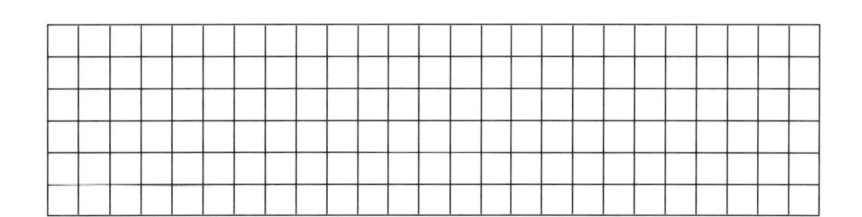

Basic Computation Series 2000: Working with Perimeter and Area
SECTION 1 Perimeter and Area of Rectangles

NAME _____   DATE _____

Finding Length, Width, Perimeter, and Area

For each rectangle, find the number of units in the length, the width, and the perimeter, and the number of square units in the area.

1. length = __11__
   width = __10__
   perimeter = __42__
   area = __110__

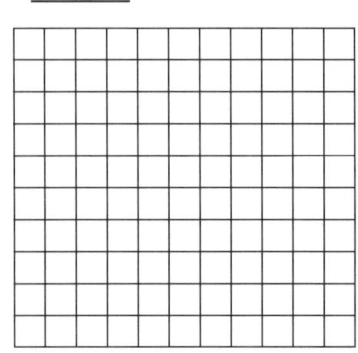

2. length = _____
   width = _____
   perimeter = _____
   area = _____

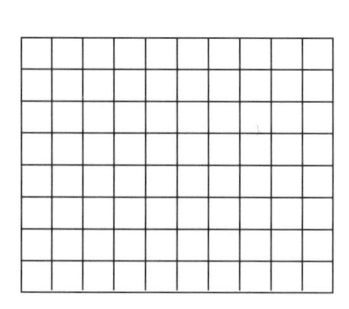

3. length = _____
   width = _____
   perimeter = _____
   area = _____

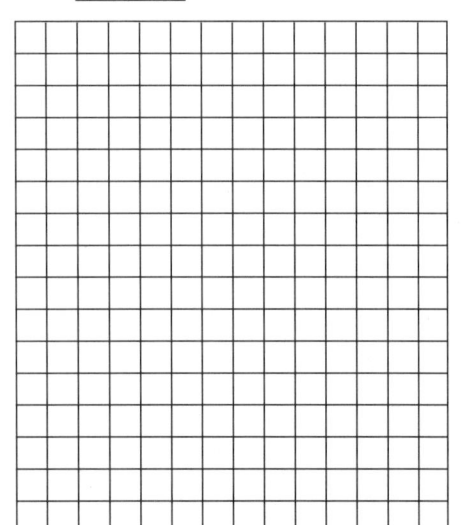

4. length = _____
   width = _____
   perimeter = _____
   area = _____

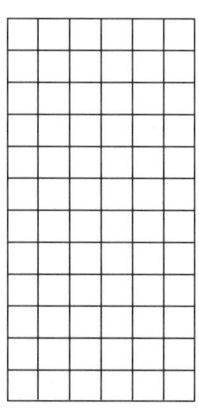

5. length = _____   width = _____   perimeter = _____   area = _____

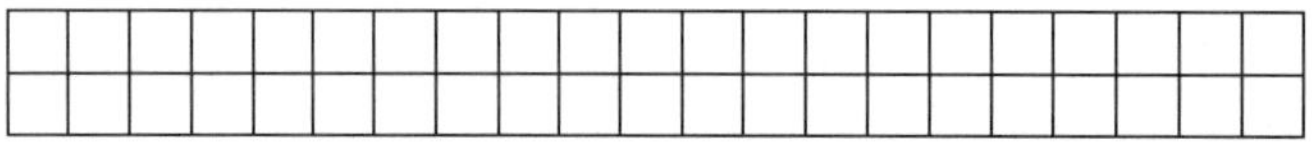

Basic Computation Series 2000: Working with Perimeter and Area
SECTION 1 Perimeter and Area of Rectangles

Finding Length, Width, Perimeter, and Area

For each rectangle, find the number of units in the length, the width, and the perimeter, and the number of square units in the area.

1. length = __12__
   width = __12__
   perimeter = __48__
   area = __144__

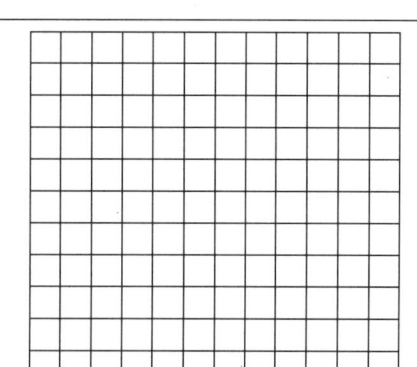

2. length = _____
   width = _____
   perimeter = _____
   area = _____

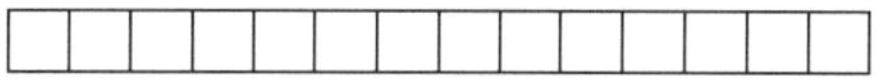

3. length = _____
   width = _____
   perimeter = _____
   area = _____

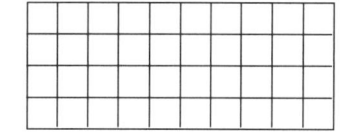

4. length = _____
   width = _____
   perimeter = _____
   area = _____

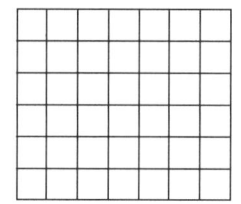

5. length = _____
   width = _____
   perimeter = _____
   area = _____

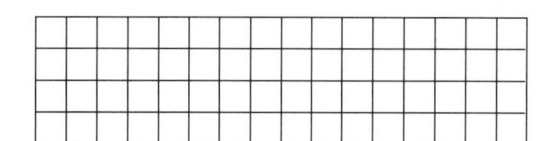

Basic Computation Series 2000: Working with Perimeter and Area
SECTION 1 Perimeter and Area of Rectangles

Drawing Rectangles with Given Area or Perimeter

For each problem, use graph paper to draw 3 different-shaped rectangles, each having the given area. Then use the chart to record the number of units in the length, the width, and the perimeter of each of your rectangles.

	first rectangle			second rectangle			third rectangle		
area	*l*	*w*	*P*	*l*	*w*	*P*	*l*	*w*	*P*
1. 12 square units	12	1	26	6	2	16	4	3	14
2. 20 square units									
3. 24 square units									
4. 18 square units									
5. 30 square units									

For each problem, use graph paper to draw 3 different-shaped rectangles, each having the given perimeter. Then use the chart to record the number of units in the length and the width, and the number of square units in the area of each of your rectangles.

	first rectangle			second rectangle			third rectangle		
perimeter	*l*	*w*	*A*	*l*	*w*	*A*	*l*	*w*	*A*
6. 30 units	10	5	50	9	6	54	8	7	56
7. 38 units									
8. 28 units									
9. 22 units									
10. 26 units									

Basic Computation Series 2000: Working with Perimeter and Area
SECTION 1 Perimeter and Area of Rectangles

NAME   DATE

Drawing Rectangles with Given Area and Perimeter

Use the graph paper below to help determine the dimensions of the rectangle that has the given perimeter and area. Record the dimensions of each rectangle in the chart.

	perimeter	area	length	width
1.	22 units	28 square units	7 units	4 units
2.	26 units	36 square units		
3.	26 units	40 square units		
4.	30 units	56 square units		
5.	28 units	45 square units		

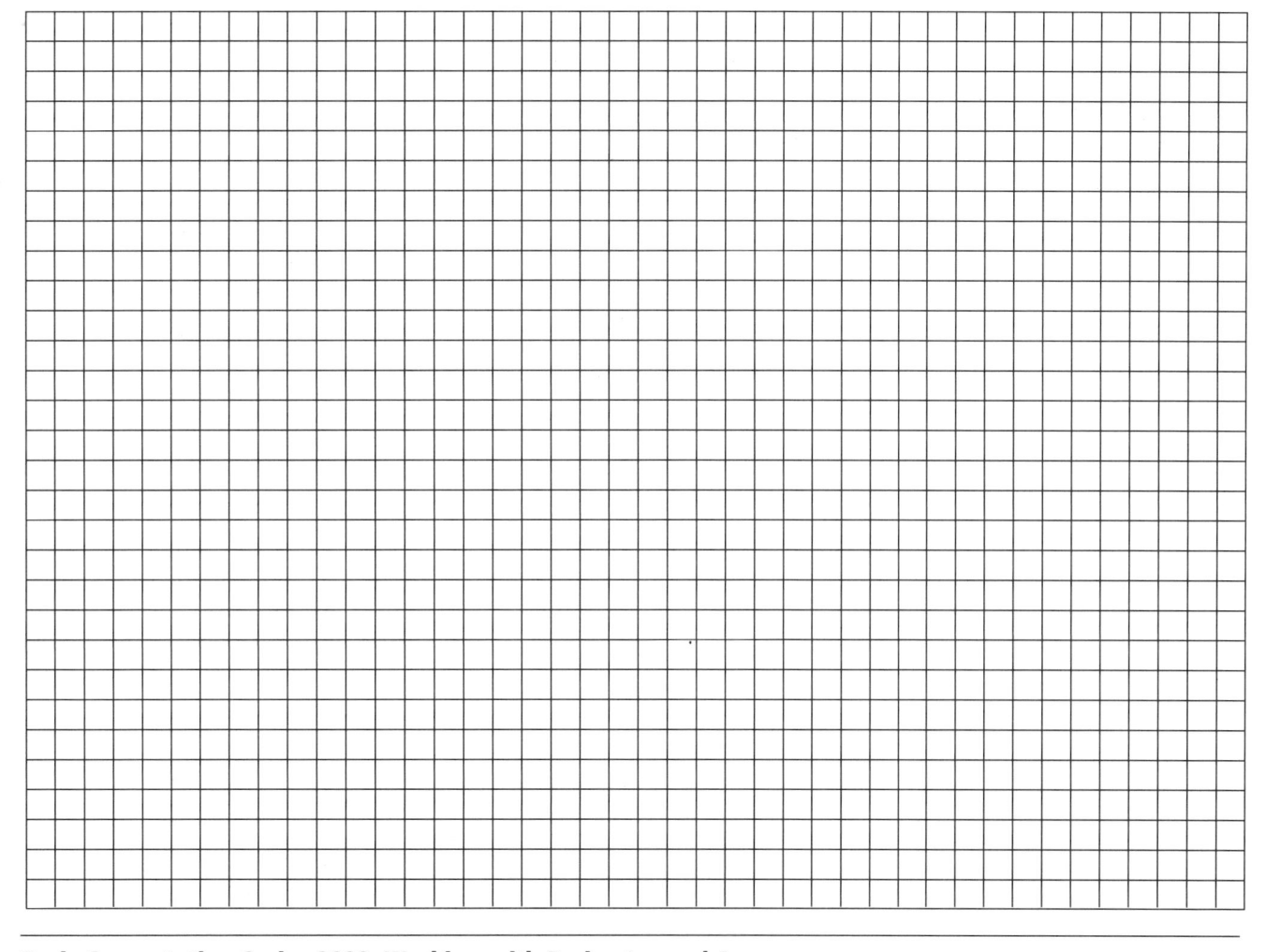

Basic Computation Series 2000: Working with Perimeter and Area

SECTION 1 Perimeter and Area of Rectangles

NAME _____ DATE _____

Drawing Rectangles with Given Area or Perimeter

For each problem, use graph paper to draw 3 different-shaped rectangles, each having the given area. Then use the chart to record the number of units in the length, the width, and the perimeter of each of your rectangles.

	first rectangle			second rectangle			third rectangle		
area	l	w	P	l	w	P	l	w	P
1. 60 square units	15	4	38	12	5	34	10	6	32
2. 100 square units									
3. 32 square units									
4. 42 square units									
5. 50 square units									

For each problem, use graph paper to draw 3 different-shaped rectangles, each having the given perimeter. Then use the chart to record the number of units in the length and the width, and the number of square units in the area of each of your rectangles.

	first rectangle			second rectangle			third rectangle		
perimeter	l	w	A	l	w	A	l	w	A
6. 40 units	19	1	19	18	2	36	17	3	51
7. 56 units									
8. 14 units									
9. 32 units									
10. 46 units									

NAME   DATE

Drawing Rectangles with Given Area and Perimeter

Use the graph paper below to help determine the dimensions of the rectangle that has the given perimeter and area. Record the dimensions of each rectangle in the chart.

	perimeter	area	length	width
1.	30 units	36 square units	12 units	3 units
2.	28 units	24 square units		
3.	36 units	45 square units		
4.	22 units	30 square units		
5.	18 units	20 square units		

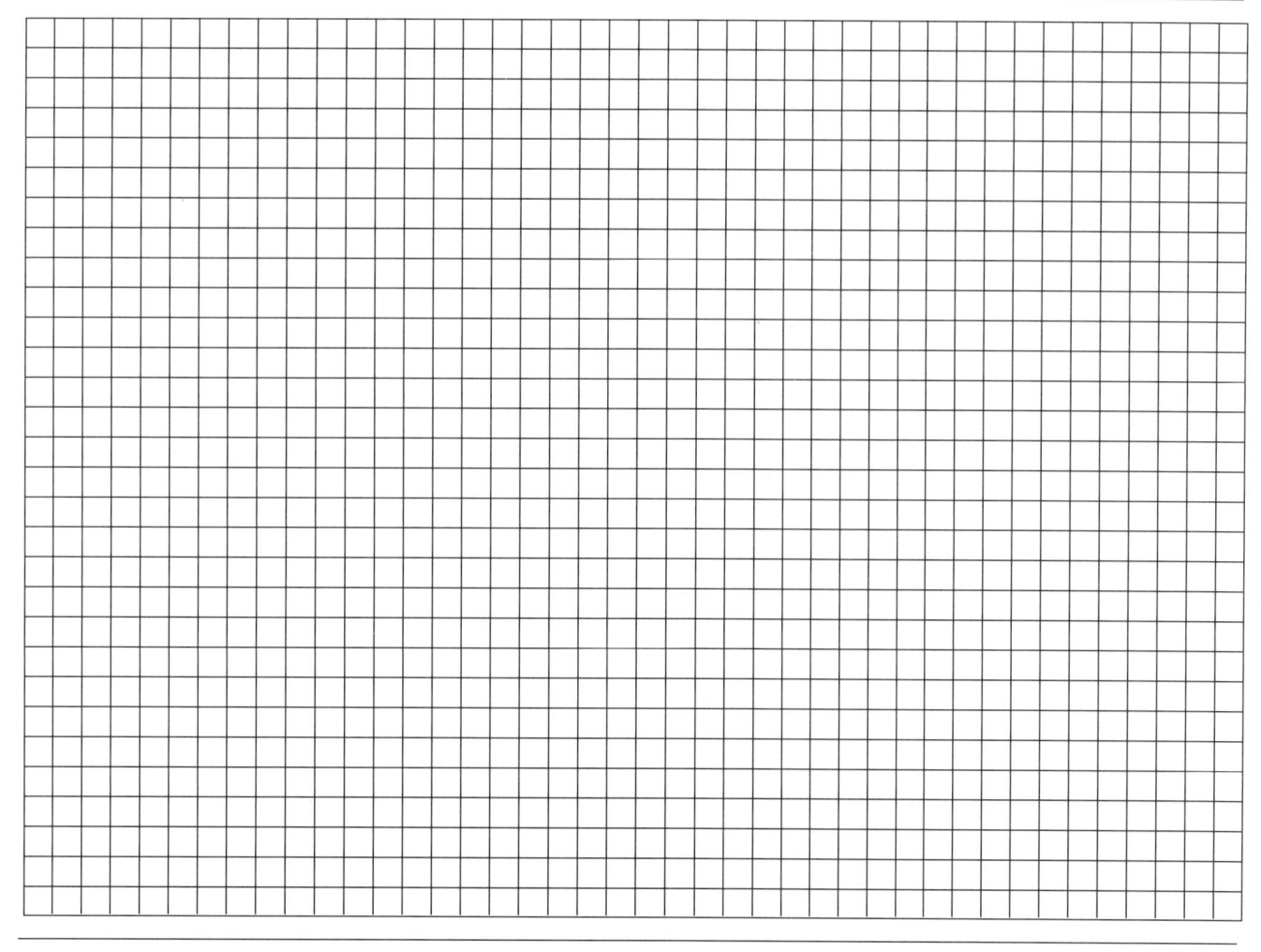

Basic Computation Series 2000: Working with Perimeter and Area
SECTION 1 Perimeter and Area of Rectangles

NAME _____   DATE _____

Drawing Rectangles with Given Area or Perimeter

For each problem, use graph paper to draw 3 different-shaped rectangles, each having the given area. Then use the chart to record the number of units in the length, the width, and the perimeter of each of your rectangles.

	first rectangle			second rectangle			third rectangle		
area	l	w	P	l	w	P	l	w	P
1. 28 square units	28	1	58	14	2	32	7	4	22
2. 64 square units									
3. 52 square units									
4. 42 square units									
5. 75 square units									

For each problem, use graph paper to draw 3 different-shaped rectangles, each having the given perimeter. Then use the chart to record the number of units in the length and the width, and the number of square units in the area of each of your rectangles.

	first rectangle			second rectangle			third rectangle		
perimeter	l	w	A	l	w	A	l	w	A
6. 18 units	8	1	8	7	2	14	5	4	20
7. 20 units									
8. 34 units									
9. 48 units									
10. 50 units									

Basic Computation Series 2000: Working with Perimeter and Area
SECTION 1 Perimeter and Area of Rectangles

Drawing Rectangles with Given Area and Perimeter

Use the graph paper below to help determine the dimensions of the rectangle that has the given perimeter and area. Record the dimensions of each rectangle in the chart.

	perimeter	area	length	width
1.	20 units	25 square units	5 units	5 units
2.	46 units	90 square units		
3.	30 units	44 square units		
4.	22 units	24 square units		
5.	34 units	60 square units		

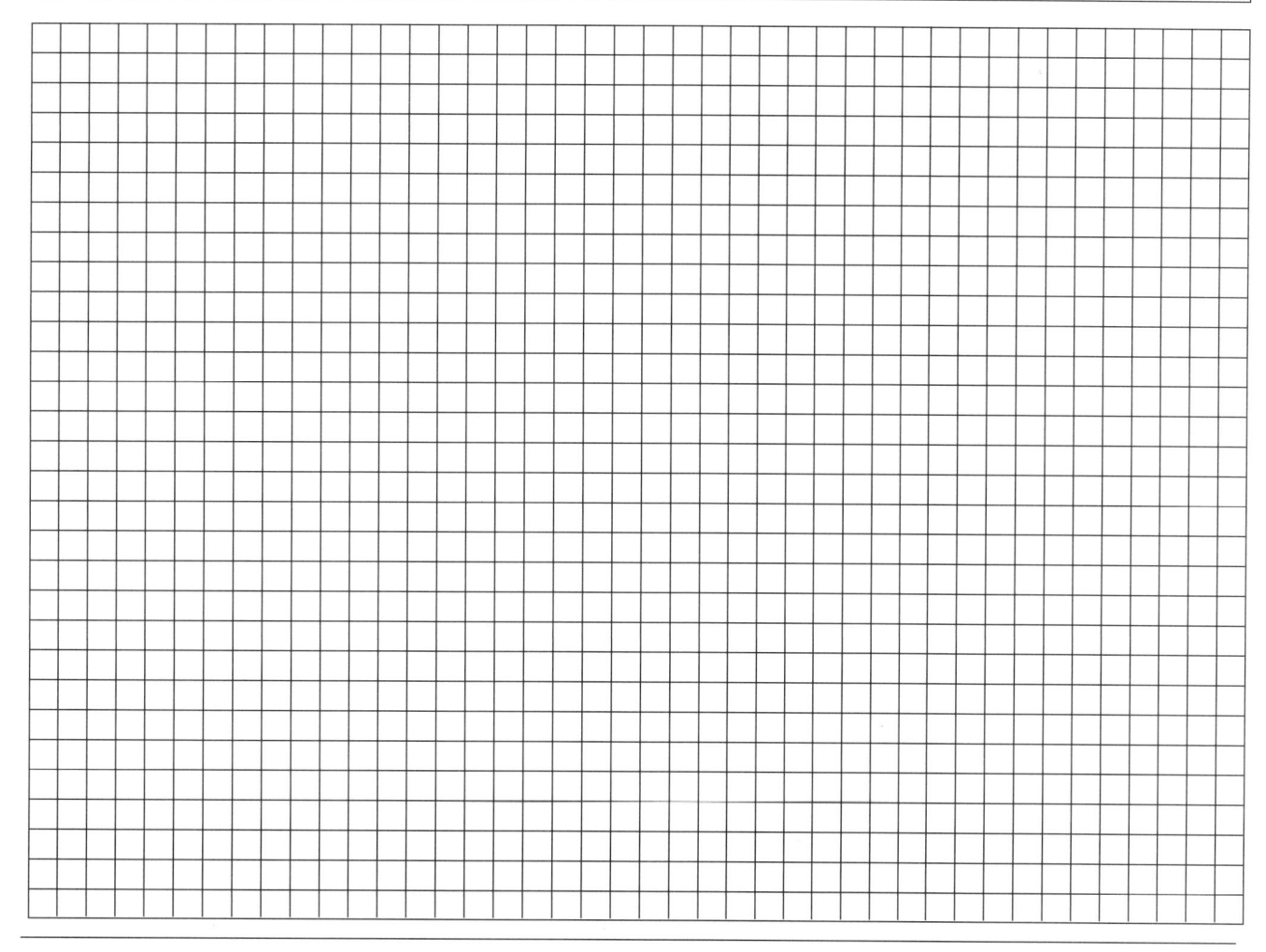

Basic Computation Series 2000: Working with Perimeter and Area

SECTION 1 Perimeter and Area of Rectangles

Drawing Rectangles with Given Area or Perimeter

For each problem, use graph paper to draw 3 different-shaped rectangles, each having the given area. Then use the chart to record the number of units in the length, the width, and the perimeter of each of your rectangles.

	first rectangle			second rectangle			third rectangle		
area	l	w	P	l	w	P	l	w	P
1. 36 square units	36	1	74	18	2	40	9	4	26
2. 30 square units									
3. 40 square units									
4. 72 square units									
5. 54 square units									

For each problem, use graph paper to draw 3 different-shaped rectangles, each having the given perimeter. Then use the chart to record the number of units in the length and the width, and the number of square units in the area of each of your rectangles.

	first rectangle			second rectangle			third rectangle		
perimeter	l	w	A	l	w	A	l	w	A
6. 16 units	7	1	7	6	2	12	5	3	15
7. 24 units									
8. 36 units									
9. 28 units									
10. 32 units									

Basic Computation Series 2000: Working with Perimeter and Area

SECTION 1 Perimeter and Area of Rectangles

Drawing Rectangles with Given Area and Perimeter

Use the graph paper below to help determine the dimensions of the rectangle that has the given perimeter and area. Record the dimensions of each rectangle in the chart.

	perimeter	area	length	width
1.	46 units	60 square units	20 units	3 units
2.	36 units	81 square units		
3.	24 units	36 square units		
4.	48 units	80 square units		
5.	38 units	84 square units		

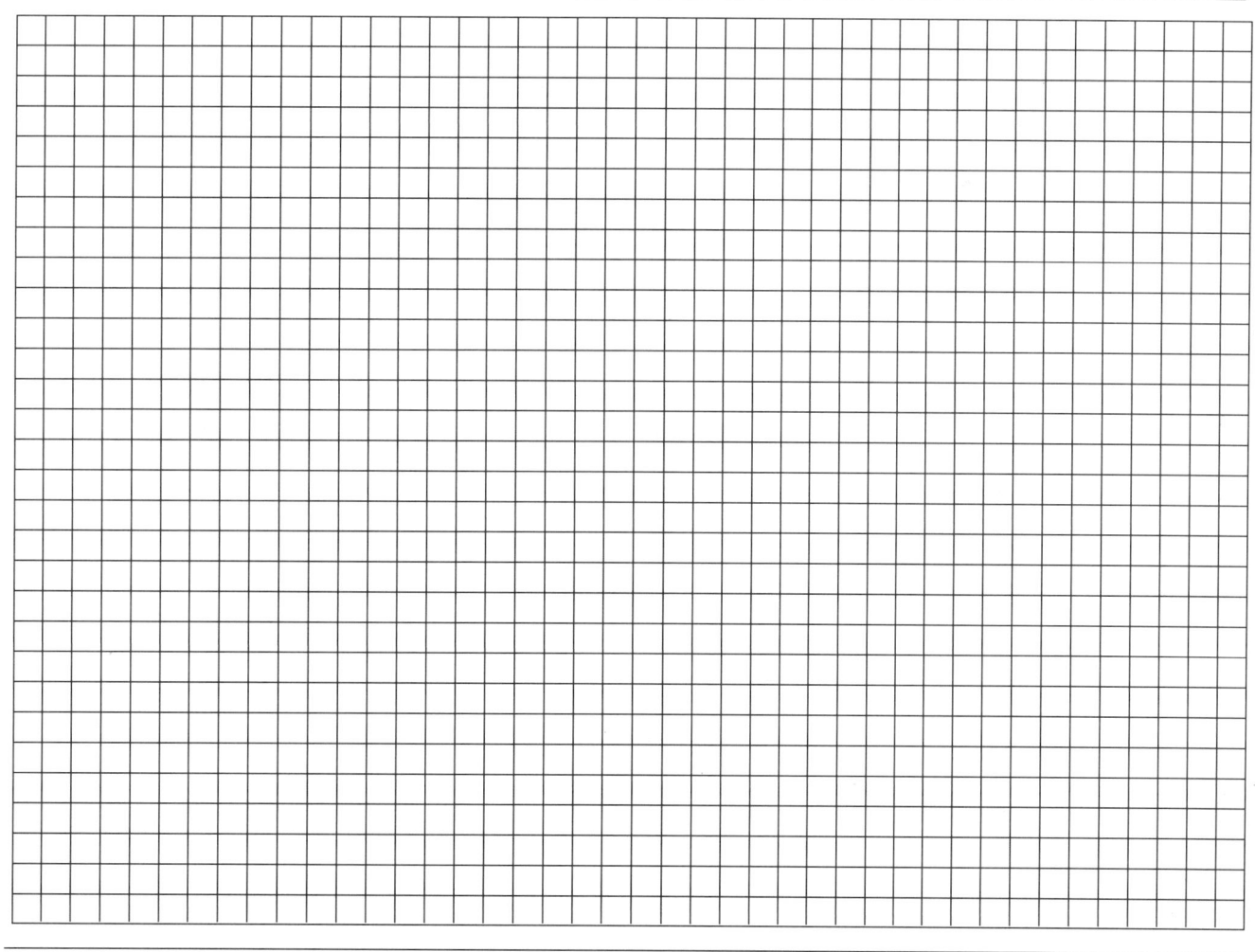

Basic Computation Series 2000: Working with Perimeter and Area
SECTION 1 Perimeter and Area of Rectangles

NAME   DATE

Drawing Rectangles with Given Area or Perimeter

For each problem, use graph paper to draw 3 different-shaped rectangles, each having the given area. Then use the chart to record the number of units in the length, the width, and the perimeter of each of your rectangles.

	first rectangle			second rectangle			third rectangle		
area	l	w	P	l	w	P	l	w	P
1. 20 square units	20	1	42	10	2	24	5	4	18
2. 45 square units									
3. 32 square units									
4. 56 square units									
5. 18 square units									

For each problem, use graph paper to draw 3 different-shaped rectangles, each having the given perimeter. Then use the chart to record the number of units in the length and the width, and the number of square units in the area of each of your rectangles.

	first rectangle			second rectangle			third rectangle		
perimeter	l	w	A	l	w	A	l	w	A
6. 12 units	5	1	5	4	2	8	3	3	9
7. 18 units									
8. 22 units									
9. 42 units									
10. 14 units									

Basic Computation Series 2000: Working with Perimeter and Area

SECTION 1 Perimeter and Area of Rectangles

Drawing Rectangles with Given Area and Perimeter

Use the graph paper below to help determine the dimensions of the rectangle that has the given perimeter and area. Record the dimensions of each rectangle in the chart.

	perimeter	area	length	width
1.	26 units	40 square units	8 units	5 units
2.	20 units	24 square units		
3.	32 units	64 square units		
4.	30 units	56 square units		
5.	20 units	16 square units		

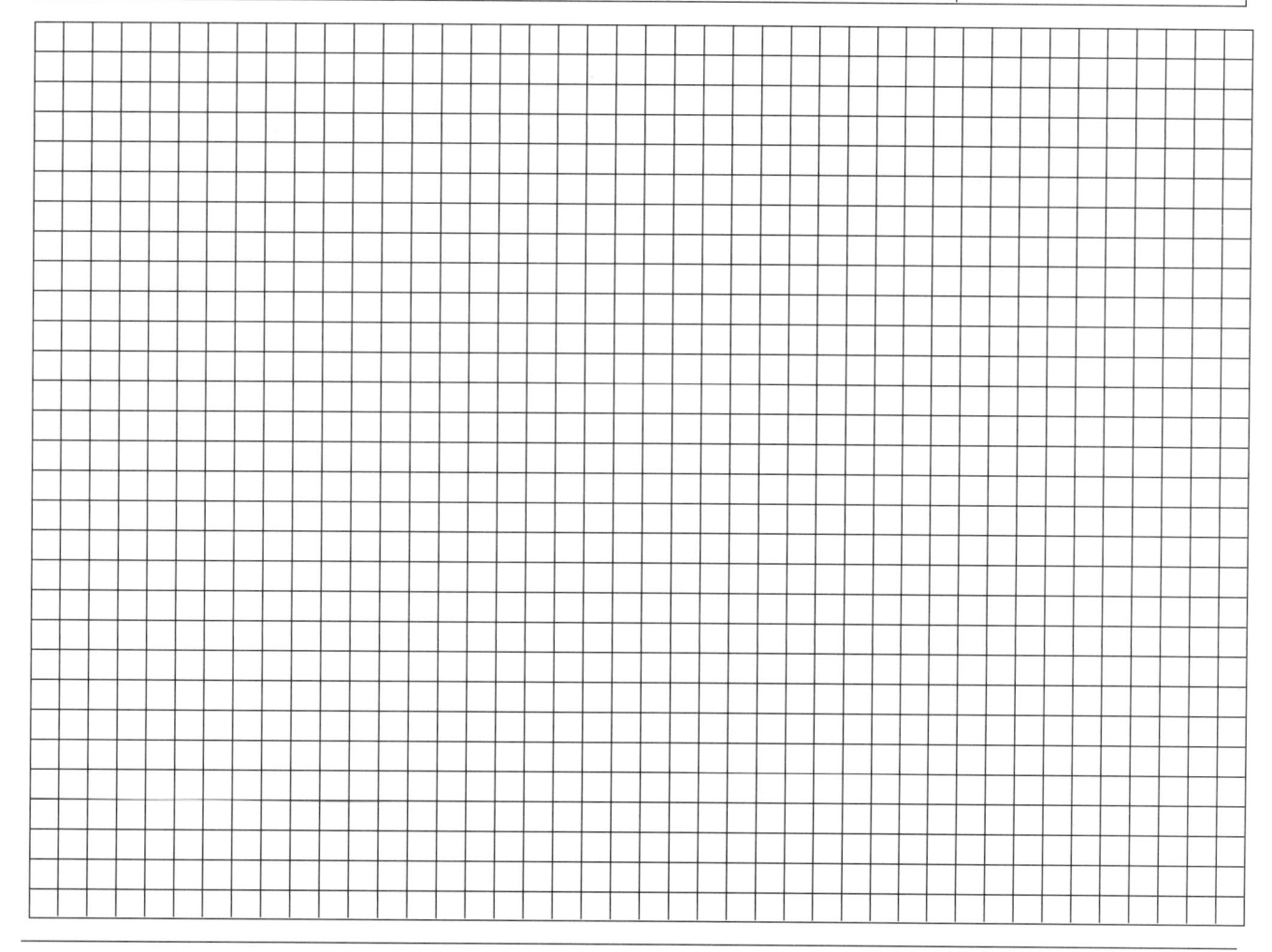

Basic Computation Series 2000: Working with Perimeter and Area
SECTION 1 Perimeter and Area of Rectangles

Perimeter and Area of Rectangles – English and Metric Units

SECTION 2

Most often, the dimensions of a rectangle are given in either English or metric units. The perimeter and area can be found using the formulas discussed in Section 1.

$$P = 2l + 2w \qquad A = l \times w$$

Recall that perimeter is measured in linear units, and area is measured in square units.

Example 1: Find the perimeter and area of a rectangle with length 12 feet and width 7 feet.

Solution: Substitute 12 for l and 7 for w.

$$P = 2 \times 12 + 2 \times 7 \qquad A = 12 \times 7$$
$$P = 38 \qquad\qquad\qquad A = 84$$

Thus, the perimeter is 38 feet and the area is 84 square feet.

Rather than writing "square feet," it is convenient to use the abbreviation "sq. ft." It is even more convenient to use an exponent and write "ft^2." In this book, an exponent is used in answers that contain square units.

When finding the perimeter and area of rectangles, the units of measure for the dimensions must be the same. If they are not the same, one of them must be converted to the other. There is no convention as to which dimension should be changed; it is rather a matter of convenience. (Note: Conversion factors are discussed in Book 6, *Understanding Measurement*.)

Example 2: Find the perimeter and area of a rectangle with length 4 ft and width 1 yd.

Solution: Before using the formulas, change one dimension so the units will be the same. The arithmetic will be easier if the yards are converted to feet. Since there are 3 feet in 1 yard, the width is 3 ft. Substitute 4 for l and 3 for w in the formulas for perimeter and area.

$$P = 2 \times 4 + 2 \times 3 \qquad A = 4 \times 3$$
$$P = 14 \qquad\qquad\qquad A = 12$$

Thus, the perimeter is 14 ft and the area is 12 ft^2.

Example 3: Find the perimeter and area of a rectangle with length 21 cm and width 16 cm.

Solution: Substitute 21 for *l* and 16 for *w*.

$P = 2 \times 21 + 2 \times 16$ $A = 21 \times 16$
$P = 74$ $A = 336$

Thus, the perimeter is 74 cm and the area is 336 cm^2.

Example 4: Find the perimeter and area of a rectangle with length 17 cm and width 15 mm.

Solution: The dimensions must contain the same units. 17 cm can be changed to 170 mm. Substitute 170 for *l* and 15 for *w*.

$P = 2 \times 170 + 2 \times 15$ $A = 170 \times 15$
$P = 370$ $A = 2,550$

Thus, the perimeter is 370 mm and the area is 2,550 mm^2.

An alternate formula for perimeter of a rectangle is $P = 2 \times (l + w)$; that is, add the length and width and multiply that sum by 2. In other words, the perimeter of a rectangle is twice the sum of the length and the width.

Example 5: Find the width and area of a rectangle with length 24 in. and perimeter 82 in.

Solution: Divide the perimeter of the rectangle by 2 to find the sum of the length and width. 82 ÷ 2 = 41. Thus, the sum of the length and width is 41 in. The width is the difference between 41 and 24. Thus, the width is 17 in. To find the area, substitute 24 for *l* and 17 for *w*.

$A = 24 \times 17$
$A = 408$

Thus, the area is 408 in.^{2}

Example 6: Find the width and perimeter of a rectangle with length 43 cm and area 528.9 cm^2.

Solution: Since the area is the product of the length and width, the width is the area divided by the length. 528.9 ÷ 43 = 12.3. Thus, the width is 12.3 cm. To find the perimeter, substitute 43 for *l* and 12.3 for *w* in either perimeter formula.

$P = 2 \times 43 + 2 \times 12.3$
$P = 110.6$

Thus, the perimeter is 110.6 cm.

Perimeter and Area of Rectangles – English Units

Calculate the perimeter and area of the rectangles with the given dimensions. In problems marked *, be sure to convert the dimensions to the same units.

	length	width	perimeter	area
1.	12 ft	24 ft	72 ft	288 ft²
2.	35 yd	10 yd		
3.	35 in.	49 in.		
4.*	27 yd	24 ft		
5.*	12 ft	8 ft 6 in.		

Basic Computation Series 2000: Working with Perimeter and Area
SECTION 2 Perimeter and Area of Rectangles – English and Metric Units

NAME _____ DATE _____

Perimeter and Area of Rectangles – Metric Units

Calculate the perimeter and area of the rectangles with the given dimensions.
In problems marked *, be sure to convert the dimensions to the same units.

	length	width	perimeter	area
1.	1.9 m	0.26 m	4.32 m	0.494 m^2
2.	1.7 m	0.32 m		
3.*	2.3 cm	32 m		
4.*	2.5 km	410 m		
5.*	16 mm	0.27 cm		

Perimeter and Area of Rectangles – English Units

Calculate the perimeter and area of the rectangles with the given dimensions. In problems marked *, be sure to convert the dimensions to the same units.

	length	width	perimeter	area
1.	35 in.	18 in.	106 in.	630 in.²
2.	22 ft	17 ft		
3.*	8 ft	96 in.		
4.*	9 ft	8 ft 4 in.		
5.*	8 ft	5 ft 3 in.		

Basic Computation Series 2000: Working with Perimeter and Area
SECTION 2 Perimeter and Area of Rectangles – English and Metric Units

NAME _____ DATE _____

Perimeter and Area of Rectangles – Metric Units

Calculate the perimeter and area of the rectangles with the given dimensions.
In problems marked *, be sure to convert the dimensions to the same units.

	length	width	perimeter	area
1.	9.3 dm	7.2 dm	33 dm	66.96 dm²
2.	87 cm	92 cm		
3.*	3.6 m	120 cm		
4.*	12.2 dkm	2.5 m		
5.*	11.4 m	1.25 cm		

30

Basic Computation Series 2000: Working with Perimeter and Area
SECTION 2 Perimeter and Area of Rectangles – English and Metric Units

NAME _____ DATE _____

Perimeter and Area of Rectangles – English Units

Calculate the perimeter and area of the rectangles with the given dimensions. In problems marked *, be sure to convert the dimensions to the same units.

	length	width	perimeter	area
1.	12 ft	8 ft	40 ft	96 ft²
2.	15 ft	9 ft		
3.*	9 ft 3 in.	12 ft		
4.*	6 yd	7 yd 8 in.		
5.*	17 in.	2 ft		

Basic Computation Series 2000: Working with Perimeter and Area
SECTION 2 Perimeter and Area of Rectangles – English and Metric Units

Perimeter and Area of Rectangles – Metric Units

Calculate the perimeter and area of the rectangles with the given dimensions.
In problems marked *, be sure to convert the dimensions to the same units.

	length	width	perimeter	area
1.	1.7 dm	5.3 dm	14 dm	9.01 dm²
2.*	4.3 m	12 dm		
3.*	8.6 cm	1.2 mm		
4.*	15 dkm	23 m		
5.*	14 m	0.023 mm		

Basic Computation Series 2000: Working with Perimeter and Area
SECTION 2 Perimeter and Area of Rectangles – English and Metric Units

Perimeter and Area of Rectangles – English Units

Calculate the perimeter and area of the rectangles with the given dimensions.
In problems marked *, be sure to convert the dimensions to the same units.

	length	width	perimeter	area
1.	14 in.	17 in.	62 in.	238 in.²
2.*	12 ft	5 ft 6 in.		
3.*	35 ft	14 yd		
4.*	13 ft	5 yd		
5.*	15 ft 2 in.	18 ft		

Basic Computation Series 2000: Working with Perimeter and Area
SECTION 2 Perimeter and Area of Rectangles – English and Metric Units

NAME _____ DATE _____

Perimeter and Area of Rectangles – Metric Units

Calculate the perimeter and area of the rectangles with the given dimensions.
In problems marked *, be sure to convert the dimensions to the same units.

	length	width	perimeter	area
1.	9.2 dm	8.7 dm	35.8 dm	80.04 dm²
2.*	4.3 m	28 dm		
3.*	2.9 cm	85 mm		
4.*	23 cm	8.1 m		
5.*	6.5 m	23 cm		

Basic Computation Series 2000: Working with Perimeter and Area
SECTION 2 Perimeter and Area of Rectangles – English and Metric Units

NAME   DATE

Perimeter and Area of Rectangles – English Units

Calculate the perimeter and area of the rectangles with the given dimensions. In problems marked *, be sure to convert the dimensions to the same units.

	length	width	perimeter	area
1.	43 in.	25 in.	136 in.	1,075 in.^{2}
2.	96 ft	73 ft		
3.*	19 yd	27 ft		
4.*	28 ft	6 ft 6 in.		
5.*	16 ft	58 ft 3 in.		

Basic Computation Series 2000: Working with Perimeter and Area
SECTION 2 Perimeter and Area of Rectangles – English and Metric Units

Perimeter and Area of Rectangles – Metric Units

Calculate the perimeter and area of the rectangles with the given dimensions. In problems marked *, be sure to convert the dimensions to the same units.

	length	width	perimeter	area
1.	1.6 cm	0.28 cm	3.76 cm	0.448 cm^2
2.	5.9 mm	8.6 mm		
3.*	13.2 m	125 cm		
4.*	6.5 dm	63 cm		
5.*	82 m	0.43 cm		

NAME DATE

Working with Perimeter and Area Formulas – English Units

Complete the following table.

	length	width	perimeter	area
1.	30 ft	8 ft	76 ft	240 ft²
2.	32 yd	12 yd		
3.	72 in.	16 in.		
4.	27 in.	14 in.		
5.	62 ft	15 ft		
6.	$4\frac{1}{4}$ mi	$6\frac{2}{5}$ mi		
7.	5 ft 3 in.	5 ft 4 in.		
8.	19 in.			494 in.²
9.	29 ft			522 ft²
10.		14 ft	238 ft	
11.		36 yd	328 yd	

Basic Computation Series 2000: Working with Perimeter and Area
SECTION 2 Perimeter and Area of Rectangles – English and Metric Units

NAME _____ DATE _____

Working with Perimeter and Area Formulas – Metric Units

Complete the following table.

length	width	perimeter	area
1. 12.3 cm	9.2 cm	43 cm	113.16 cm²
2. 7.32 m	4.01 m		
3.	3.2 m		18.24 m²
4. 69 mm			278.07 mm²
5. 3.5 cm		12.2 cm	
6. 8.7 m		36 m	
7. 46 cm			190.44 cm²

Basic Computation Series 2000: Working with Perimeter and Area
SECTION 2 Perimeter and Area of Rectangles – English and Metric Units

Working with Perimeter and Area Formulas – English Units

Complete the following table.

	length	width	perimeter	area
1.	15 ft	5 ft	40 ft	75 ft²
2.	16 in.	12 in.		
3.	40 yd	20 yd		
4.	23 ft	15 ft		
5.	17 in.	32 in.		
6.	3 ft 4 in.	2 ft 3 in.		
7.	6 yd 1 ft	7 yd 18 in.		
8.	19 ft			133 ft²
9.	26 in.			312 in.²
10.		24 yd	118 yd	
11.	57 ft		178 ft	

Basic Computation Series 2000: Working with Perimeter and Area
SECTION 2 Perimeter and Area of Rectangles – English and Metric Units

NAME

DATE

Working with Perimeter and Area Formulas – Metric Units

Complete the following table.

	length	width	perimeter	area
1.	83 cm	72 cm	310 cm	5,976 cm²
2.	57 mm	36 mm		
3.	10.3 m	8.2 m		
4.	5.7 dm	3.4 dm		
5.	4.8 m			12.48 m²
6.	5.11 cm			18.3449 cm²
7.		3.9 m	18.6 m	

Working with Perimeter and Area Formulas – English Units

Complete the following table.

	length	width	perimeter	area
1.	12 yd	4 yd	32 yd	48 yd²
2.	45 ft	15 ft		
3.	32 ft	27 ft		
4.	53 yd	36 yd		
5.	9 ft 4 in.	3 ft 9 in.		
6.	7 ft 2 in.	5 ft 3 in.		
7.	5 yd 9 in.	9 yd 12 in.		
8.	23 in.			414 in.²
9.	36 in.			972 in.²
10.	47 ft		156 ft	
11.		$5\frac{1}{2}$ ft	22 ft	

Basic Computation Series 2000: Working with Perimeter and Area

SECTION 2 Perimeter and Area of Rectangles – English and Metric Units

NAME

DATE

Working with Perimeter and Area Formulas – Metric Units

Complete the following table.

	length	width	perimeter	area
1.	34 cm	16 cm	100 cm	544 cm^2
2.	43 cm	67 cm		
3.	92 m	23 m		
4.	1.32 mm	4.8 mm		
5.	92 cm			5,612 cm^2
6.	5.6 m			24.08 m^2
7.	43 mm		158 mm	

Basic Computation Series 2000: Working with Perimeter and Area

SECTION 2 Perimeter and Area of Rectangles – English and Metric Units

Working with Perimeter and Area Formulas – English Units

Complete the following table.

	length	width	perimeter	area
1.	28 ft	13 ft	82 ft	364 ft²
2.	58 ft	16 ft		
3.	72 in.	34 in.		
4.	57 yd	26 yd		
5.	10 ft 6 in.	7 ft 4 in.		
6.	6 ft 8 in.	4 ft 9 in.		
7.	9 yd 9 in.	11 yd 12 in.		
8.	43 in.			1,204 in.²
9.	67 in.			2,881 in.²
10.		14 in.	82 in.	
11.	15 ft		40 ft	

Basic Computation Series 2000: Working with Perimeter and Area

SECTION 2 Perimeter and Area of Rectangles – English and Metric Units

Working with Perimeter and Area Formulas – Metric Units

Complete the following table.

	length	width	perimeter	area
1.	15 m	5 m	40 m	75 m²
2.	24 cm	12 cm		
3.	37 cm	2.9 cm		
4.		51 cm		3,723 cm²
5.		63 mm		6,048 mm²
6.	77 cm		222 cm	
7.	38 mm		128 mm	

NAME   DATE

Working with Perimeter and Area Formulas – English Units

Complete the following table.

	length	width	perimeter	area
1.	48 ft	12 ft	120 ft	576 ft²
2.	37 in.	19 in.		
3.	39 in.	29 in.		
4.	76 ft	32 ft		
5.	125 yd	14 yd		
6.	5 ft 4 in.	2 ft 3 in.		
7.	3 ft 4 in.	4 ft 3 in.		
8.	7 yd 2 ft	3 yd 1 ft		
9.	29 in.			377 in.²
10.	86 ft			2,064 ft²
11.		33 in.		561 in.²

Basic Computation Series 2000: Working with Perimeter and Area
SECTION 2 Perimeter and Area of Rectangles – English and Metric Units

Working with Perimeter and Area Formulas – Metric Units

Complete the following table.

	length	width	perimeter	area
1.	58 mm	26 mm	168 mm	1,508 mm^2
2.	18.2 cm	7.5 cm		
3.	0.927 m	1.3 m		
4.	8.6 mm	5.32 mm		
5.	92 cm			3,174 cm^2
6.	69 m		544 m	
7.	62 mm		178 mm	

Perimeter and Area of Triangles, Parallelograms, and Trapezoids

SECTION 3

A triangle has three sides and three angles. The sides may be named a, b, and c, and the angles may be named A, B, and C, with side a opposite angle A, side b opposite angle B, and side c opposite angle C. A triangle has a base (b) and height (h) as shown in the figure below. Although the height of a triangle can be measured from any of the three vertices perpendicular to the opposite side, the heights of the triangles in this book will be measured to side b so that side b and base b are one and the same. The formula for the area, A, of a triangle is $A = \frac{1}{2} \times b \times h$, which, written more simply, is $A = \frac{1}{2}bh$. The formula for perimeter, P, is $P = a + b + c$.

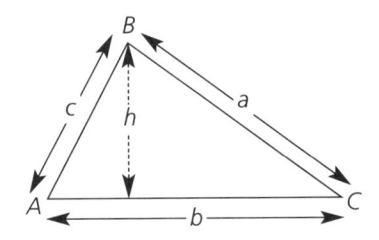

In some triangles, the height is actually the length of a side of the triangle. Consider a right triangle like the one shown below. In a right triangle, two sides are perpendicular to each other; therefore, one is the base and the other is the height measured to that base. In the figure, side b is the base, and side a, the height. The formulas for area and perimeter are as above; however, an alternate form of the perimeter formula is $P = h + b + c$.

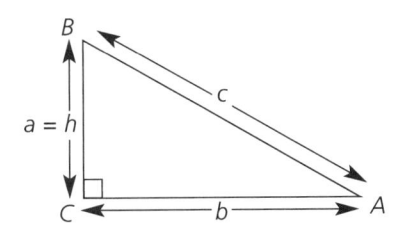

Example 1: Find the number of units in the base and height of the right triangle shown, and the number of square units in its area.

Solution: Count the number of units to find that b = 8 and h = 5. $A = \frac{1}{2} \times 8 \times 5$. Thus, the area is 20 square units.

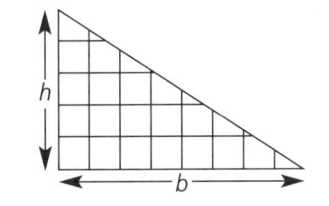

Basic Computation Series 2000: Working with Perimeter and Area

Example 2: Use graph paper to draw 3 different-shaped right triangles, each with area 18 square units. (Note: A blackline master for graph paper is provided on page 94.)

Solution: Since the area of the triangle must be 18 square units, the product of the base and height must be 36. If the dimensions are to be whole numbers of units, the possible combinations are:

$b = 36$ and $h = 1$
$b = 18$ and $h = 2$
$b = 12$ and $h = 3$
$b = 6$ and $h = 6$

Except for interchanging the values of b and h, no other possibilities exist. Three possible triangles are shown below.

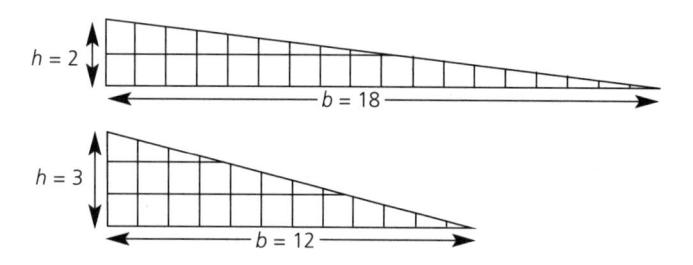

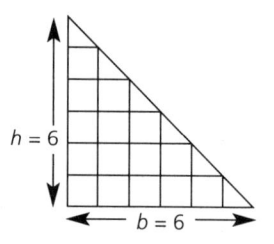

Example 3: Find the area and perimeter of a right triangle in which $b = 4$ ft, $h = 3$ ft, and $c = 5$ ft.

Solution: $A = \frac{1}{2} \times 4 \times 3$. Thus, the area is 6 ft².
$P = 3 + 4 + 5$. Thus, the perimeter is 12 ft.

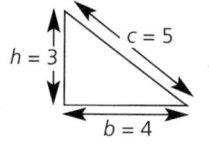

Example 4: Find the area and perimeter of a right triangle in which $b = 24$ m, $h = 10$ m, and $c = 26$ m.

Solution: $A = \frac{1}{2} \times 24 \times 10$. Thus, the area is 120 m².
$P = 10 + 24 + 26$. Thus, the perimeter is 60 m.

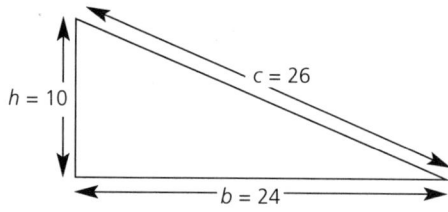

Example 5: Find the number of units in the base and height of the triangle shown below, and the number of square units in its area.

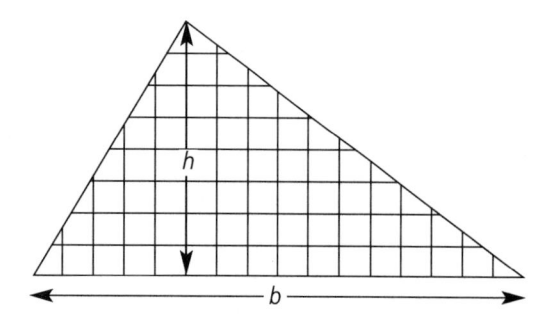

Solution: Count the squares to find that $b = 16$ and $h = 8$. $A = \frac{1}{2} \times 16 \times 8$. Thus, the area of the triangle is 64 square units.

Basic Computation Series 2000: Working with Perimeter and Area
SECTION 3 Perimeter and Area of Triangles, Parallelograms, and Trapezoids

Example 6: Use graph paper to draw 3 different-shaped triangles, each with base 6 units and altitude 3 units. Then find the area of the triangles.

Solution: Three possible triangles are shown below. In each case, $A = \frac{1}{2} \times 6 \times 3$. Thus, the area of each triangle is 9 square units.

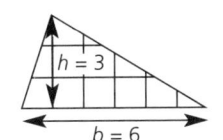

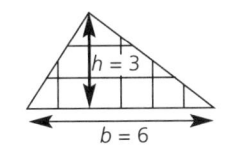

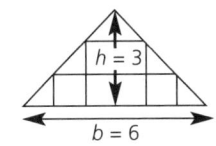

Example 7: Find the area and perimeter of a triangle in which $a = 10$ units, $b = 21$ units, $c = 17$ units, and $h = 8$ units.

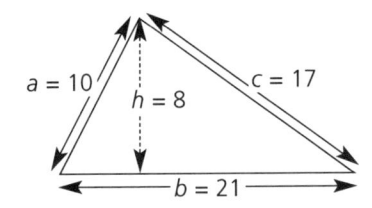

Solution: $A = \frac{1}{2} \times 21 \times 8$. Thus, the area is 84 units^2.
$P = 10 + 21 + 17$. Thus, the perimeter is 48 units.

A parallelogram is a four-sided figure in which opposite sides are parallel. As shown in the figure below, opposite sides are also the same length. The height (h) of the parallelogram is the distance between opposite sides.

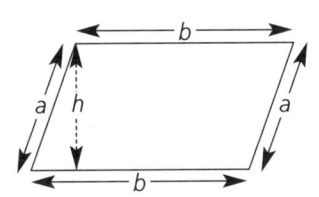

If the lengths of the sides are as shown in the figure, then the formula for the perimeter of the parallelogram is $P = a + b + a + b$ or, written more simply, $P = 2a + 2b$, or $P = 2(a + b)$. If the base measures b units and the height measures h units, the formula for the area of the parallelogram is $A = bh$.

Example 8: Find the area and perimeter of the parallelogram shown if $a = 61$ units, $b = 81$ units, and $h = 60$ units.

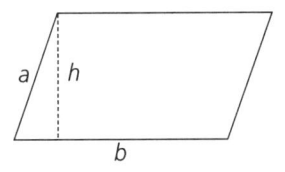

Solution: $A = 81 \times 60$. Thus, the area is 4,860 units^2.
$P = 2 \times 61 + 2 \times 81$. Thus, the perimeter is 284 units

Basic Computation Series 2000: Working with Perimeter and Area
SECTION 3 Perimeter and Area of Triangles, Parallelograms, and Trapezoids

A trapezoid is a four-sided figure in which only two sides are parallel. In the figure below, the parallel sides are labeled b_1 and b_2 because they are both considered bases but they are not the same length. The non-parallel sides are labeled a and c.

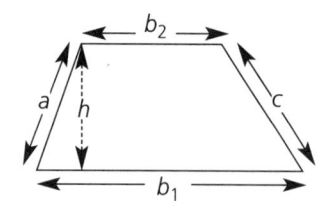

The perimeter of a trapezoid is the sum of the lengths of its sides; that is, $P = a + b_1 + b_2 + c$. The formula for the area of a trapezoid is $A = \frac{1}{2} h (b_1 + b_2)$. To apply this formula, add the bases together, multiply by the height, and multiply the result by $\frac{1}{2}$.

Example 9: Find the perimeter and area of the trapezoid shown if $a = 34$ units, $b_1 = 98$ units, $b_2 = 42$ units, $c = 50$ units, and $h = 30$ units.

Solution: $A = \frac{1}{2}(30)(98 + 42)$. Thus, the area is 2,100 units^2.
$P = 34 + 98 + 42 + 50$. Thus, the perimeter is 224 units.

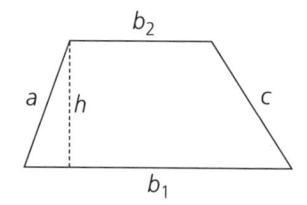

Basic Computation Series 2000: Working with Perimeter and Area
SECTION 3 Perimeter and Area of Triangles, Parallelograms, and Trapezoids

NAME DATE

Area of Right Triangles

For each right triangle, find the number of units in the base and height, and the number of square units in the area.

1. base = __11__
   height = __4__
   area = __22__

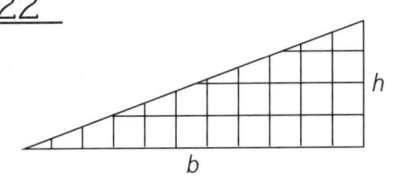

2. base = _____
   height = _____
   area = _____

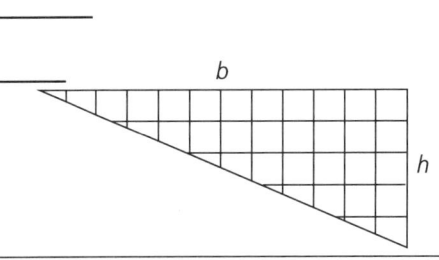

3. base = _____
   height = _____
   area = _____

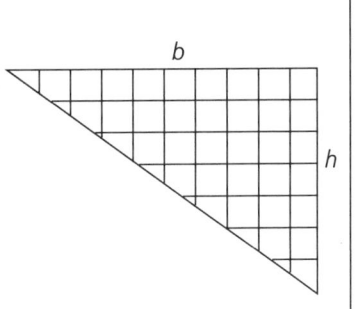

4. base = _____
   height = _____
   area = _____

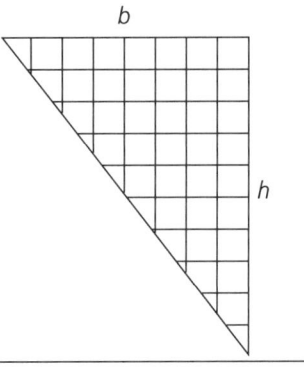

5. base = _____
   height = _____
   area = _____

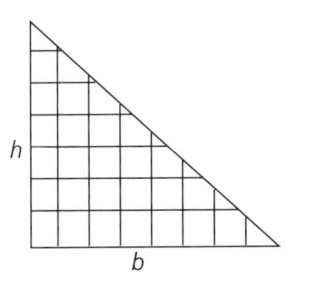

6. base = _____
   height = _____
   area = _____

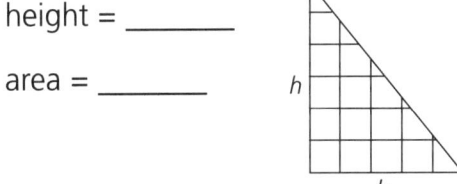

7. base = _____
   height = _____
   area = _____

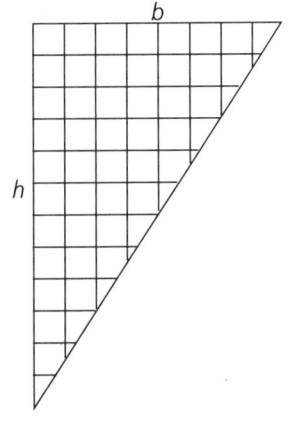

8. base = _____
   height = _____
   area = _____

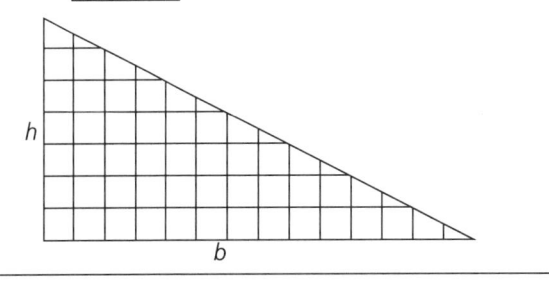

Basic Computation Series 2000: Working with Perimeter and Area
SECTION 3 Perimeter and Area of Triangles, Parallelograms, and Trapezoids

NAME _____ DATE _____

Drawing Right Triangles with Given Area

1. Draw three different-shaped right triangles, each with area 36 square units. For each triangle, state the number of units in the base and the height.

   base = _____   base = _____   base = _____

   height = _____   height = _____   height = _____

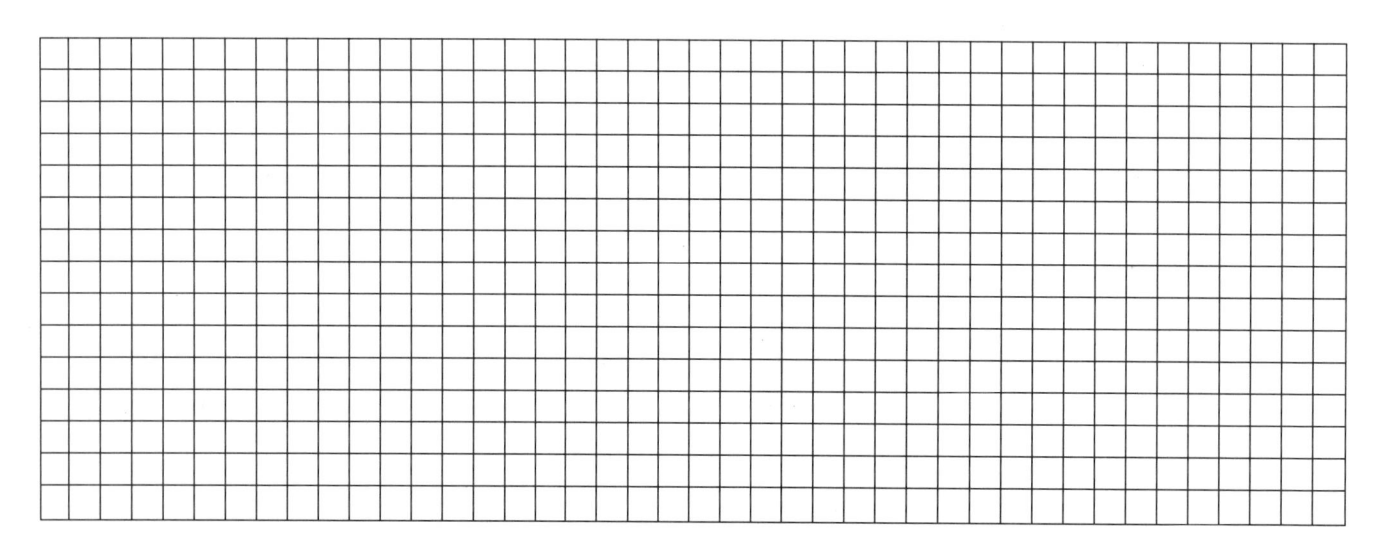

2. Draw three different-shaped right triangles, each with area 24 square units. For each triangle, state the number of units in the base and the height.

   base = _____   base = _____   base = _____

   height = _____   height = _____   height = _____

Basic Computation Series 2000: Working with Perimeter and Area
SECTION 3 Perimeter and Area of Triangles, Parallelograms, and Trapezoids

NAME DATE

Area of Right Triangles

For each right triangle, find the number of units in the base and height, and the number of square units in the area.

1. base = __11__
   height = __6__
   area = __33__

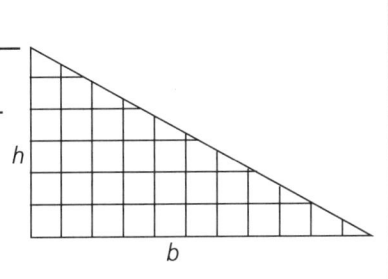

2. base = _____
   height = _____
   area = _____

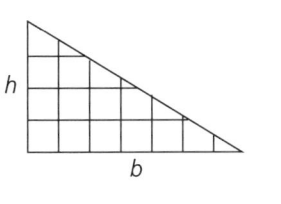

3. base = _____
   height = _____
   area = _____

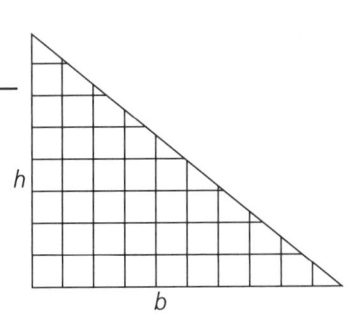

4. base = _____
   height = _____
   area = _____

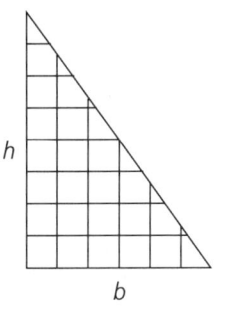

5. base = _____
   height = _____
   area = _____

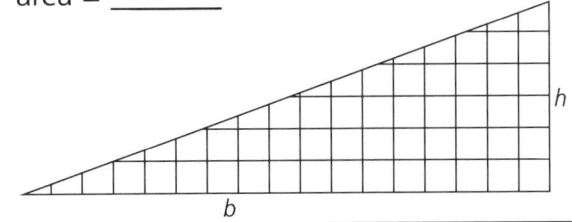

6. base = _____
   height = _____
   area = _____

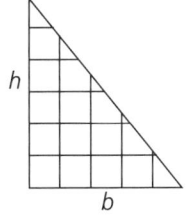

7. base = _____
   height = _____
   area = _____

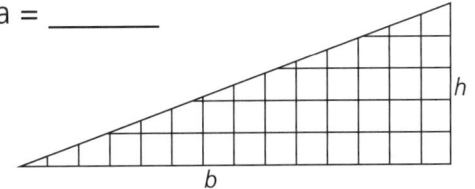

8. base = _____
   height = _____
   area = _____

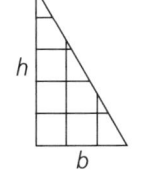

Basic Computation Series 2000: Working with Perimeter and Area
SECTION 3 Perimeter and Area of Triangles, Parallelograms, and Trapezoids

Drawing Right Triangles with Given Area

1. Draw three different-shaped right triangles, each with area 30 square units. For each triangle, state the number of units in the base and the height.

   base = _____   base = _____   base = _____

   height = _____   height = _____   height = _____

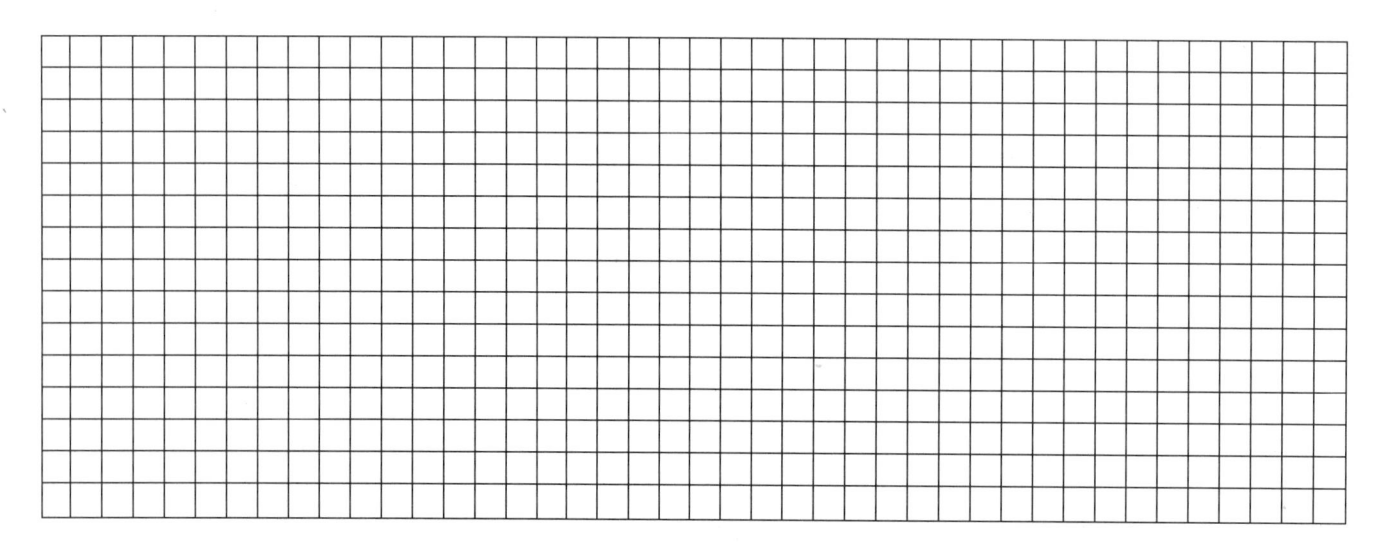

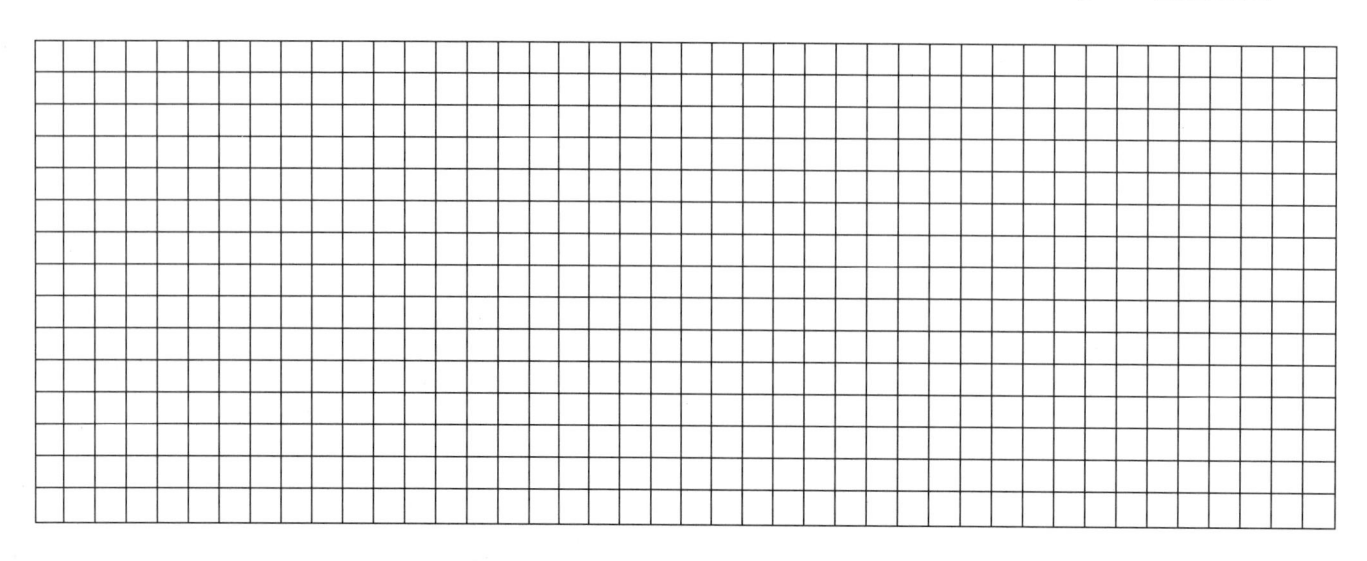

2. Draw three different-shaped right triangles, each with area 40 square units. For each triangle, state the number of units in the base and the height.

   base = _____   base = _____   base = _____

   height = _____   height = _____   height = _____

NAME   DATE

Area of Right Triangles

For each right triangle, find the number of units in the base and height, and the number of square units in the area.

1. base = __13__
   height = __6__
   area = __39__

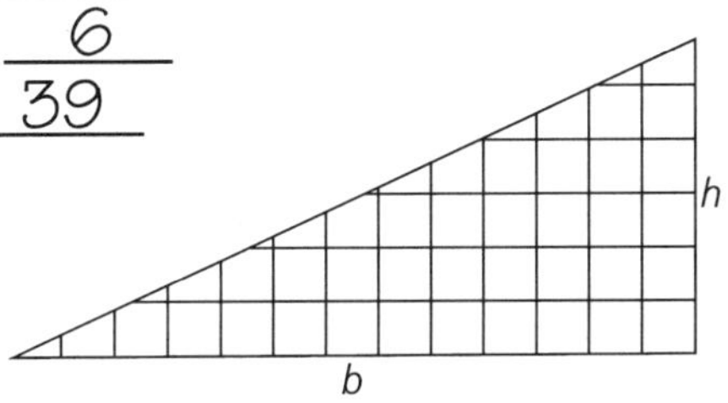

2. base = _____
   height = _____
   area = _____

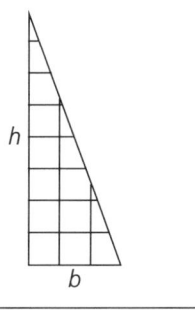

3. base = _____
   height = _____
   area = _____

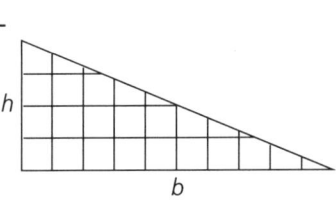

4. base = _____
   height = _____
   area = _____

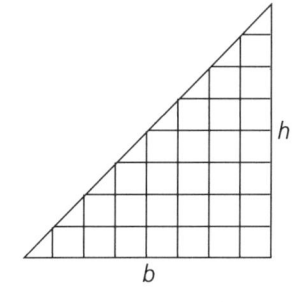

5. base = _____
   height = _____
   area = _____

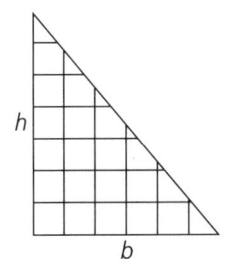

6. base = _____
   height = _____
   area = _____

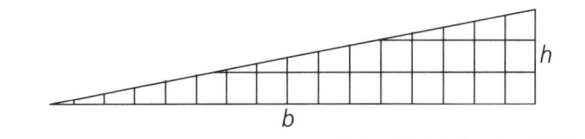

7. base = _____
   height = _____
   area = _____

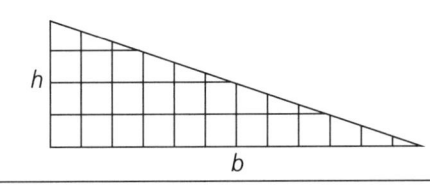

8. base = _____
   height = _____
   area = _____

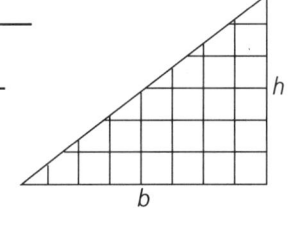

Basic Computation Series 2000: Working with Perimeter and Area
SECTION 3 Perimeter and Area of Triangles, Parallelograms, and Trapezoids

Drawing Right Triangles with Given Area

1. **Draw three different-shaped right triangles, each with area 12 square units. For each triangle, state the number of units in the base and the height.**

    base = _____   base = _____   base = _____

    height = _____   height = _____   height = _____

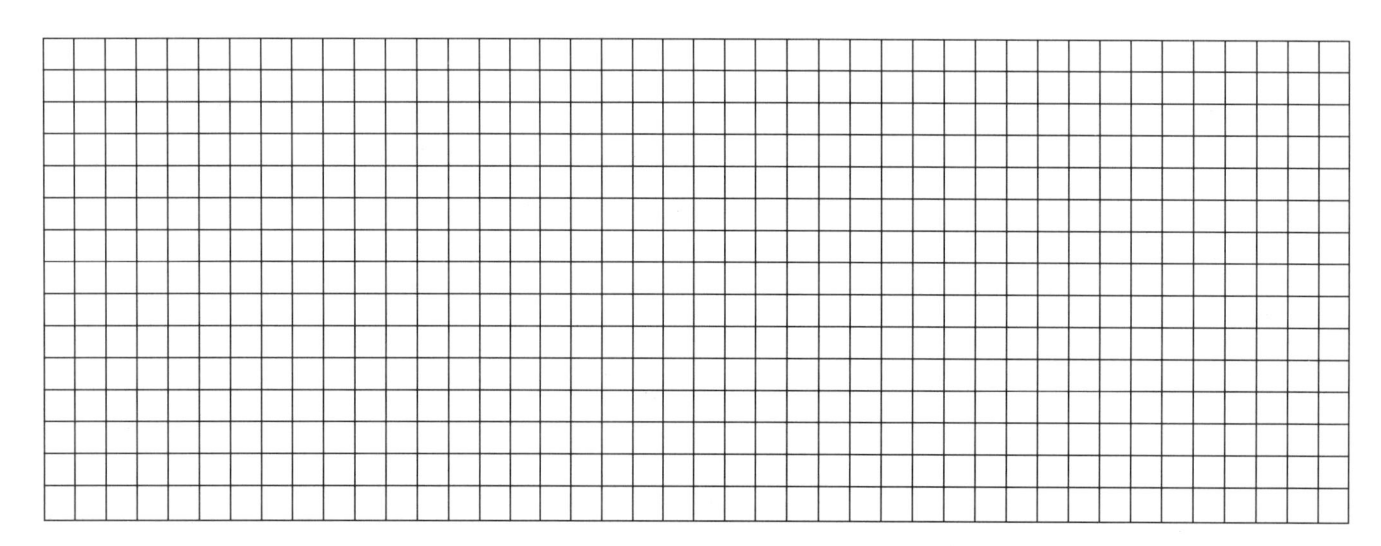

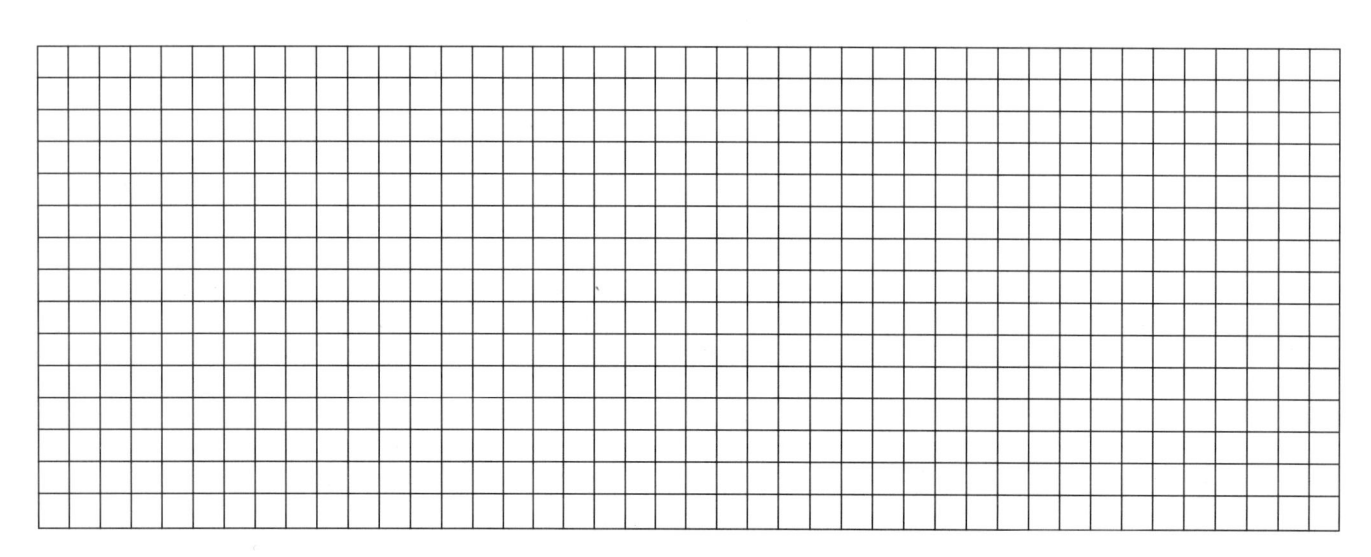

2. **Draw three different-shaped right triangles, each with area 8 square units. For each triangle, state the number of units in the base and the height.**

    base = _____   base = _____   base = _____

    height = _____   height = _____   height = _____

Basic Computation Series 2000: Working with Perimeter and Area

NAME DATE

Area of Right Triangles

For each right triangle, find the number of units in the base and height, and the number of square units in the area.

1. base = __13__
   height = __6__
   area = __39__

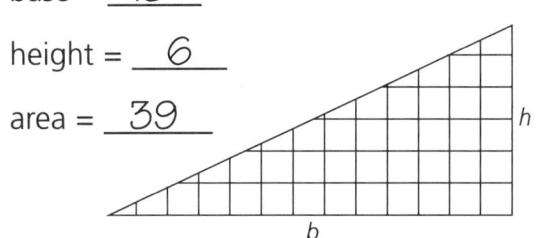

2. base = _____
   height = _____
   area = _____

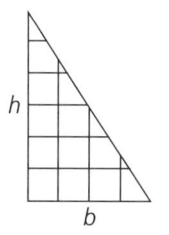

3. base = _____
   height = _____
   area = _____

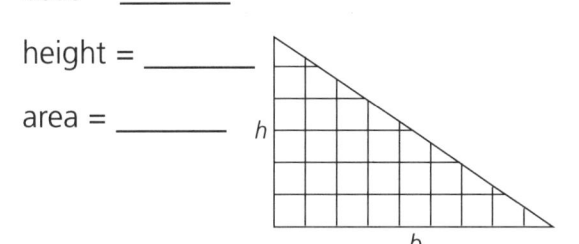

4. base = _____
   height = _____
   area = _____

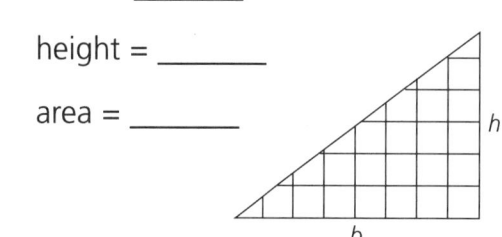

5. base = _____
   height = _____
   area = _____

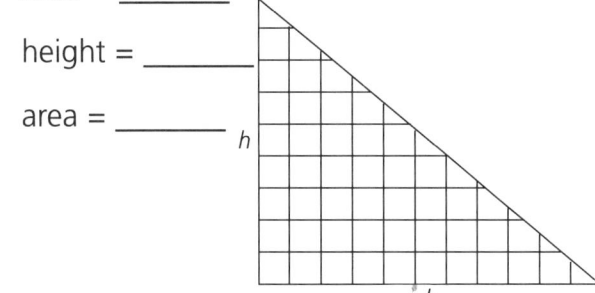

6. base = _____
   height = _____
   area = _____

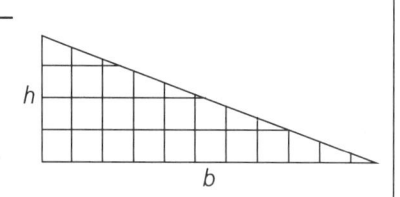

7. base = _____
   height = _____
   area = _____

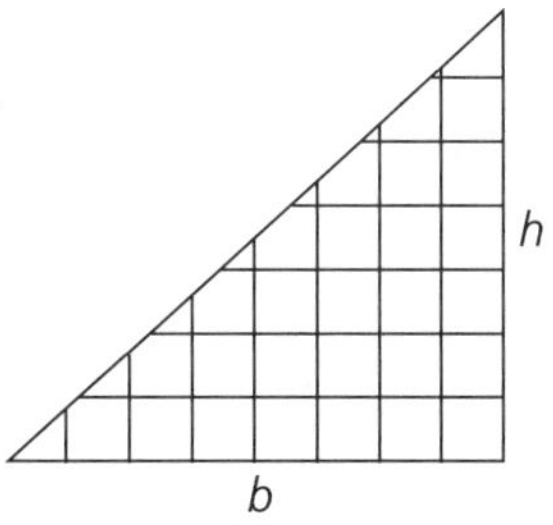

8. base = _____
   height = _____
   area = _____

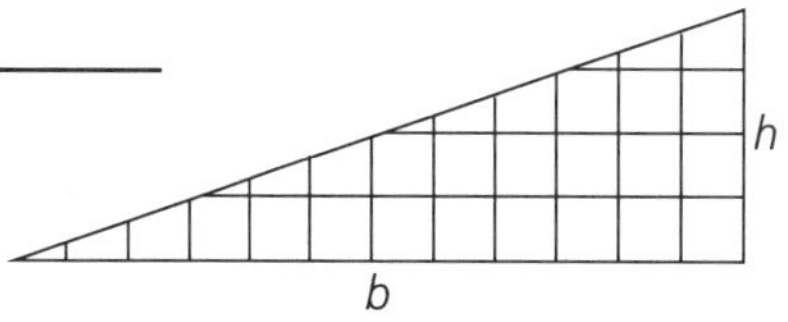

Basic Computation Series 2000: Working with Perimeter and Area
SECTION 3 Perimeter and Area of Triangles, Parallelograms, and Trapezoids

NAME _____   DATE _____

Drawing Right Triangles with Given Area

1. Draw three different-shaped right triangles, each with area 10 square units. For each triangle, state the number of units in the base and the height.

   base = _____   base = _____   base = _____

   height = _____   height = _____   height = _____

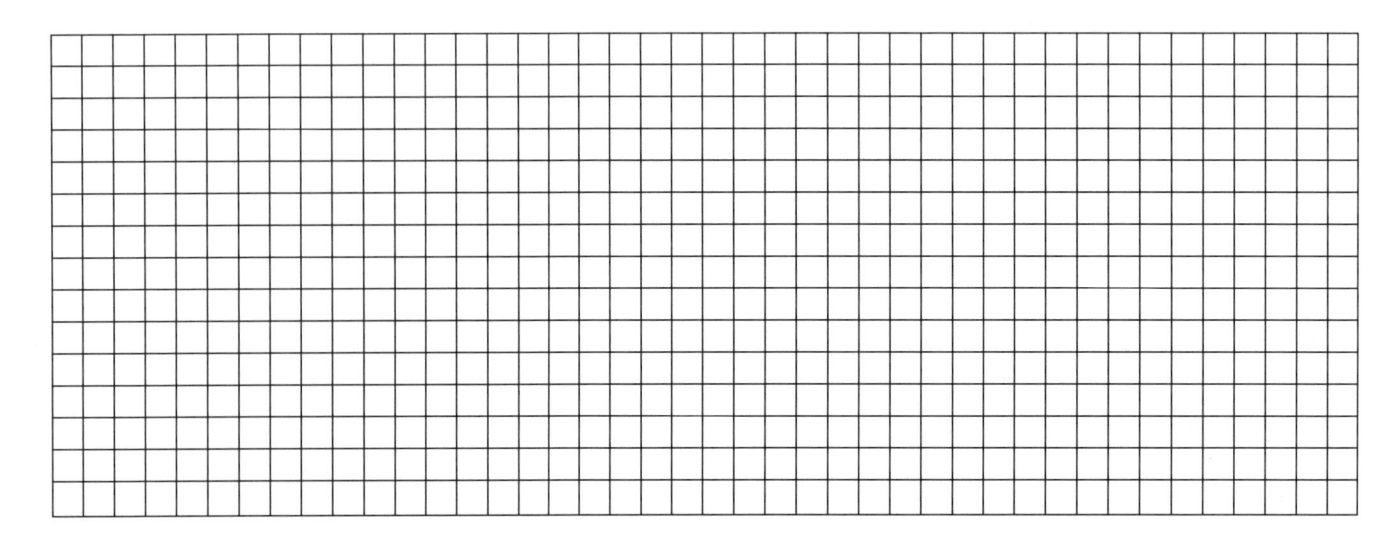

2. Draw three different-shaped right triangles, each with area 20 square units. For each triangle, state the number of units in the base and the height.

   base = _____   base = _____   base = _____

   height = _____   height = _____   height = _____

Basic Computation Series 2000: Working with Perimeter and Area

SECTION 3 Perimeter and Area of Triangles, Parallelograms, and Trapezoids

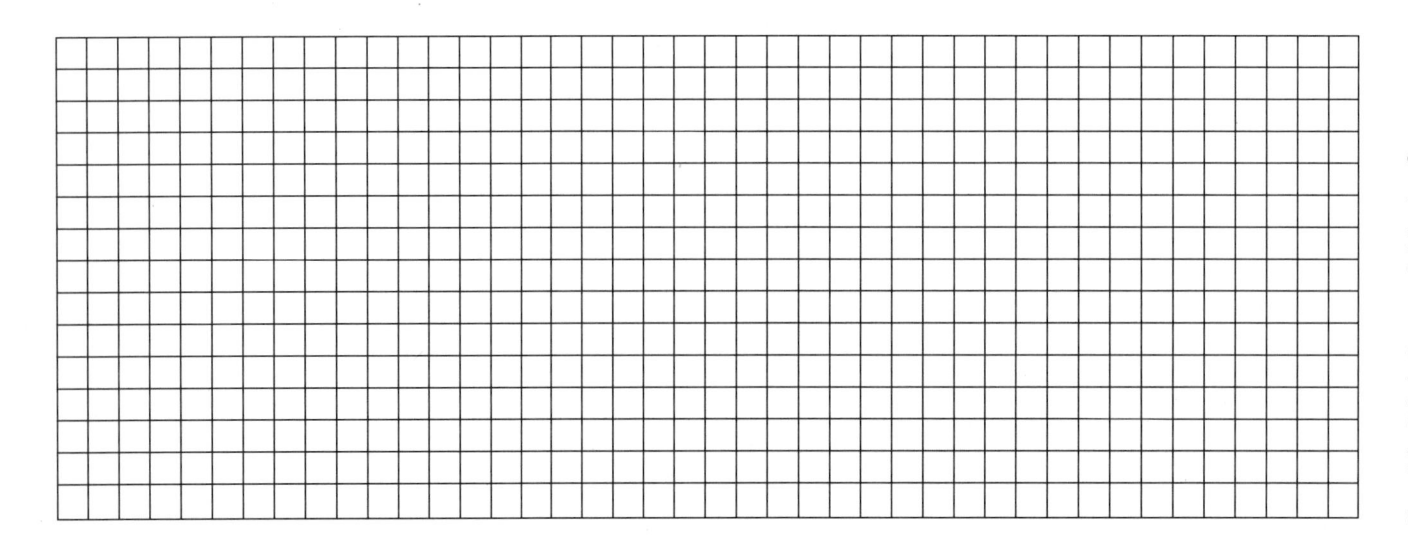

NAME DATE

Area of Right Triangles

For each right triangle, find the number of units in the base and height, and the number of square units in the area.

1. base = __11__
   height = __9__
   area = __49½__

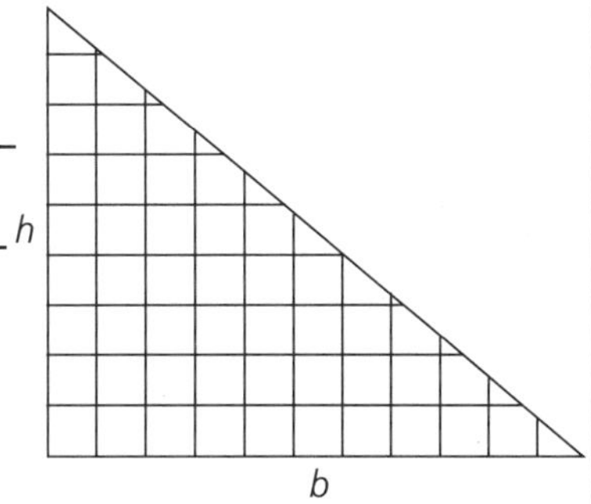

2. base = _____
   height = _____
   area = _____

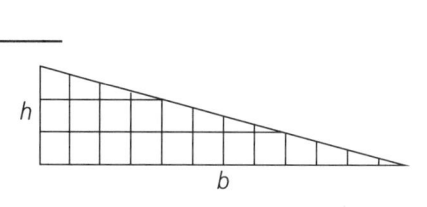

3. base = _____
   height = _____
   area = _____

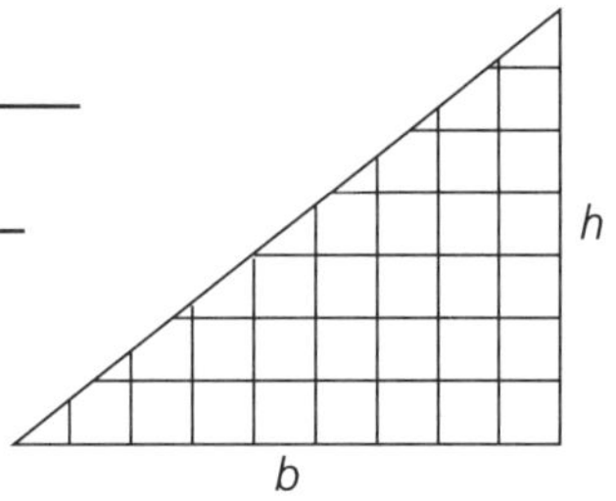

4. base = _____
   height = _____
   area = _____

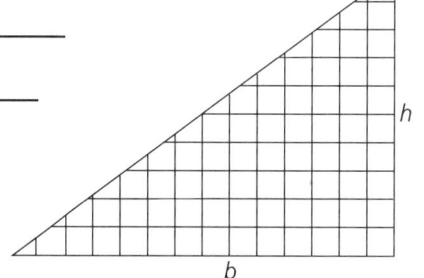

5. base = _____
   height = _____
   area = _____

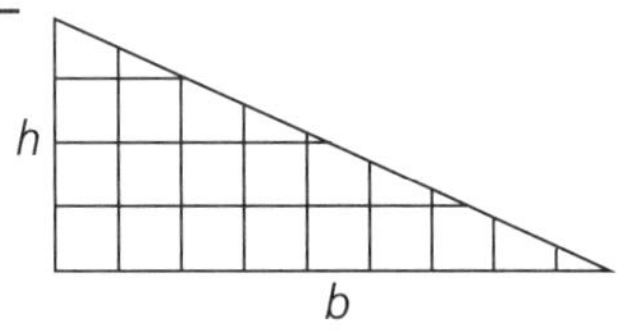

6. base = _____
   height = _____
   area = _____

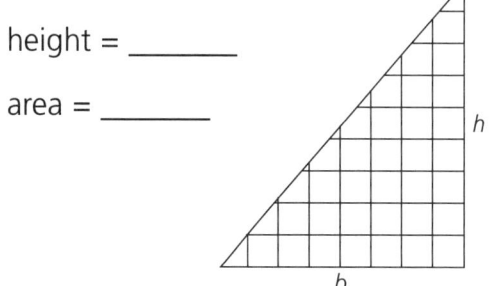

7. base = _____
   height = _____
   area = _____

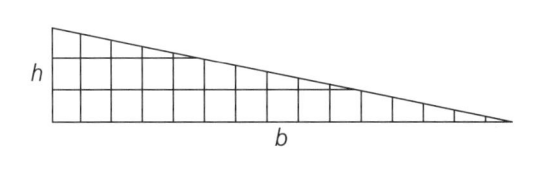

8. base = _____
   height = _____
   area = _____

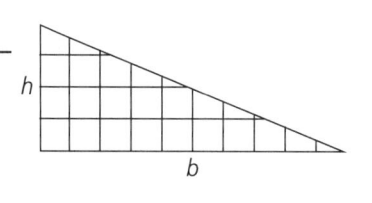

Basic Computation Series 2000: Working with Perimeter and Area
SECTION 3 Perimeter and Area of Triangles, Parallelograms, and Trapezoids

NAME _____ DATE _____

Drawing Right Triangles with Given Area

1. Draw three different-shaped right triangles, each with area 18 square units. For each triangle, state the number of units in the base and the height.

   base = _____   base = _____   base = _____

   height = _____   height = _____   height = _____

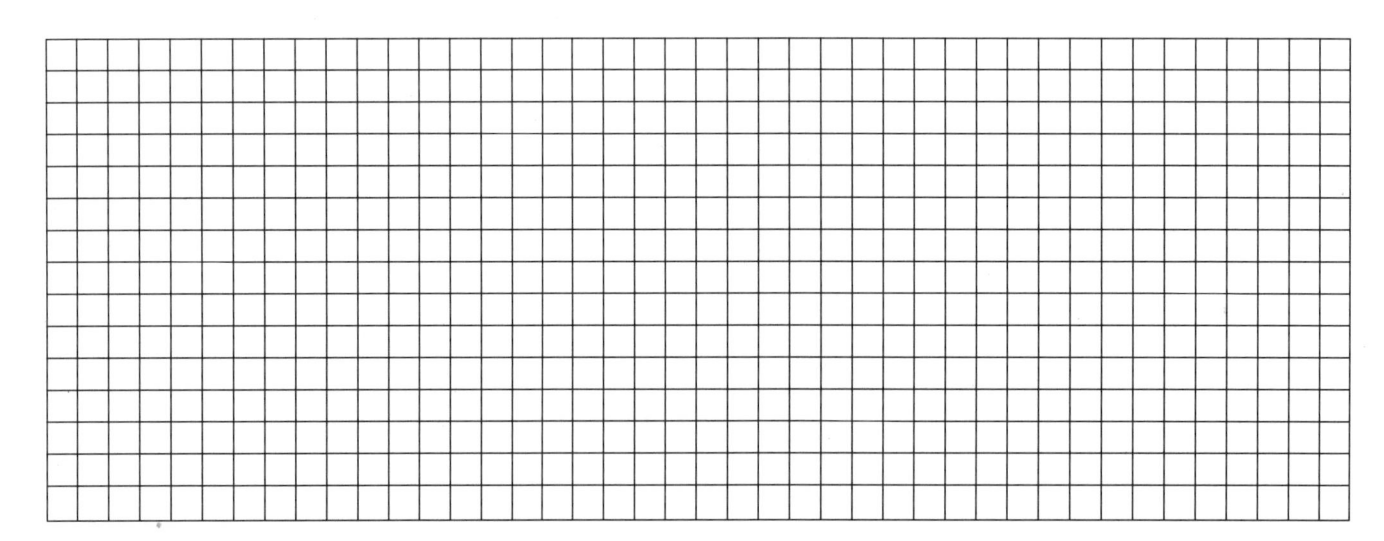

2. Draw three different-shaped right triangles, each with area 16 square units. For each triangle, state the number of units in the base and the height.

   base = _____   base = _____   base = _____

   height = _____   height = _____   height = _____

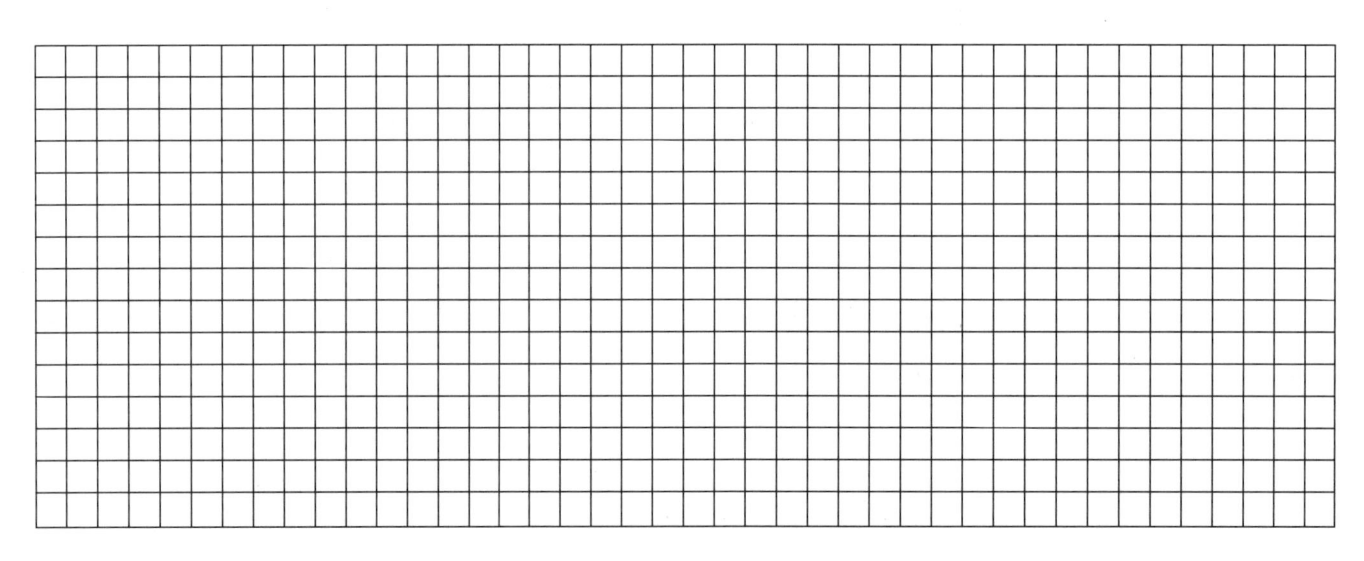

Basic Computation Series 2000: Working with Perimeter and Area

SECTION 3 Perimeter and Area of Triangles, Parallelograms, and Trapezoids

Perimeter and Area of Right Triangles – English Units

Find the perimeter and area of the right triangle shown given each set of dimensions.

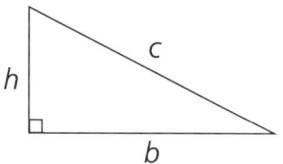

1. h = 20 in.
   b = 21 in.
   c = 29 in.
   perimeter = __70 in.__
   area = __210 in.^{2}__

2. h = 28 yd
   b = 45 yd
   c = 53 yd
   perimeter = _____
   area = _____

3. h = 48 ft
   b = 55 ft
   c = 73 ft
   perimeter = _____
   area = _____

4. h = 60 in.
   b = 91 in.
   c = 109 in.
   perimeter = _____
   area = _____

5. h = 40 yd
   b = 42 yd
   c = 58 yd
   perimeter = _____
   area = _____

Basic Computation Series 2000: Working with Perimeter and Area
SECTION 3 Perimeter and Area of Triangles, Parallelograms, and Trapezoids

Perimeter and Area of Right Triangles – Metric Units

Find the perimeter and area of the right triangle shown given each set of dimensions. In problems marked *, be sure to convert the dimensions to the same units.

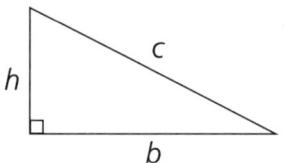

1. h = 33 km
   b = 56 km
   c = 65 km
   perimeter = __154 km__
   area = __924 km²__

2. h = 11 m
   b = 60 m
   c = 61 m
   perimeter = _____
   area = _____

3. h = 84 cm
   b = 135 cm
   c = 159 cm
   perimeter = _____
   area = _____

4.* h = 39 cm
    b = 0.8 m
    c = 8.9 dm
    perimeter = _____
    area = _____

5.* h = 0.13 m
    b = 84 cm
    c = 8.5 dm
    perimeter = _____
    area = _____

Basic Computation Series 2000: Working with Perimeter and Area
SECTION 3 Perimeter and Area of Triangles, Parallelograms, and Trapezoids

NAME _____ DATE _____

Perimeter and Area of Right Triangles – English Units

Find the perimeter and area of the right triangle shown given each set of dimensions.

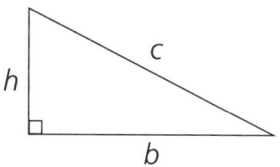

1. h = 20 ft
   b = 99 ft
   c = 101 ft
   perimeter = __220 ft__
   area = __990 ft²__

2. h = 40 in.
   b = 42 in.
   c = 58 in.
   perimeter = _____
   area = _____

3. h = 15 yd
   b = 20 yd
   c = 25 yd
   perimeter = _____
   area = _____

4. h = 36 in.
   b = 77 in.
   c = 85 in.
   perimeter = _____
   area = _____

5. h = 56 ft
   b = 33 ft
   c = 65 ft
   perimeter = _____
   area = _____

Basic Computation Series 2000: Working with Perimeter and Area
SECTION 3 Perimeter and Area of Triangles, Parallelograms, and Trapezoids

NAME _____ DATE _____

Perimeter and Area of Right Triangles – Metric Units

Find the perimeter and area of the right triangle shown given each set of dimensions. In problems marked *, be sure to convert the dimensions to the same units.

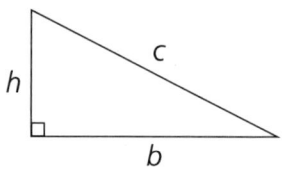

1. h = 3.3 cm
   b = 4.4 cm
   c = 5.5 cm
   perimeter = __13.2 cm__
   area = __7.26 cm²__

2. h = 4.0 m
   b = 9.6 m
   c = 10.4 m
   perimeter = _____
   area = _____

3. h = 5.6 dm
   b = 10.5 dm
   c = 11.9 dm
   perimeter = _____
   area = _____

4.* h = 6.3 m
   b = 2,160 cm
   c = 225 dm
   perimeter = _____
   area = _____

5.* h = 54 cm
   b = 2.4 m
   c = 2,460 mm
   perimeter = _____
   area = _____

Basic Computation Series 2000: Working with Perimeter and Area
SECTION 3 Perimeter and Area of Triangles, Parallelograms, and Trapezoids

NAME _____ DATE _____

Perimeter and Area of Right Triangles – English Units

Find the perimeter and area of the right triangle shown given each set of dimensions. In problems marked *, be sure to convert the dimensions to the same units.

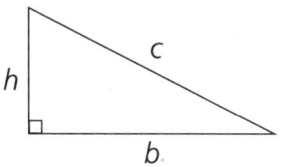

1. h = 10 ft
   b = 24 ft
   c = 26 ft
   perimeter = ___60 ft___
   area = ___120 ft²___

2. h = 27 ft
   b = 36 ft
   c = 45 ft
   perimeter = _____
   area = _____

3. h = 60 in.
   b = 144 in.
   c = 156 in.
   perimeter = _____
   area = _____

4. h = 10 yd
   b = $10\frac{1}{2}$ yd
   c = $14\frac{1}{2}$ yd
   perimeter = _____
   area = _____

5.* h = 81 ft
    b = 120 yd
    c = 123 yd
    perimeter = _____
    area = _____

Basic Computation Series 2000: Working with Perimeter and Area
SECTION 3 Perimeter and Area of Triangles, Parallelograms, and Trapezoids

NAME _____ DATE _____

Perimeter and Area of Right Triangles – Metric Units

Find the perimeter and area of the right triangle shown given each set of dimensions. In problems marked *, be sure to convert the dimensions to the same units.

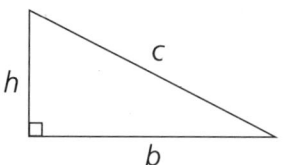

1. h = 8.4 cm
   b = 28.8 cm
   c = 30 cm
   perimeter = __67.2 cm__
   area = __120.96 cm^2__

2. h = 7.2 mm
   b = 13.5 mm
   c = 15.3 mm
   perimter = _____
   area = _____

3. h = 0.56 km
   b = 1.92 km
   c = 2 km
   perimter = _____
   area = _____

4. h = 8.8 dkm
   b = 16.5 dkm
   c = 18.7 dkm
   perimter = _____
   area = _____

5.* h = 0.45 km
   b = 600 m
   c = 750 m
   perimter = _____
   area = _____

Basic Computation Series 2000: Working with Perimeter and Area
SECTION 3 Perimeter and Area of Triangles, Parallelograms, and Trapezoids

NAME   DATE

Perimeter and Area of Right Triangles – English Units

Find the perimeter and area of the right triangle shown given each set of dimensions. In problems marked *, be sure to convert the dimensions to the same units.

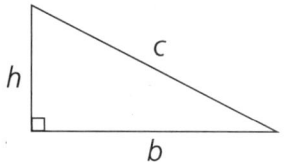

1. h = 18 in.
   b = 24 in.
   c = 30 in.
   perimeter = __72 in__
   area = __216 in.²__

2. h = 24 ft
   b = 32 ft
   c = 40 ft
   perimter = _____
   area = _____

3. h = 72 yd
   b = 320 yd
   c = 328 yd
   perimter = _____
   area = _____

4. h = 40 in.
   b = 96 in.
   c = 104 in.
   perimter = _____
   area = _____

5.* h = 14 ft
    b = 576 in.
    c = 50 ft
    perimter = _____
    area = _____

Basic Computation Series 2000: Working with Perimeter and Area
SECTION 3 Perimeter and Area of Triangles, Parallelograms, and Trapezoids

NAME _____   DATE _____

Perimeter and Area of Right Triangles – Metric Units

Find the perimeter and area of the right triangle shown given each set of dimensions. In problems marked *, be sure to convert the dimensions to the same units.

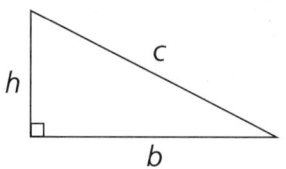

1. h = 5.4 m
   b = 7.2 m
   c = 9 m
   perimeter = __21.6 m__
   area = __19.44 m²__

2. h = 0.7 km
   b = 1.68 km
   c = 1.82 km
   perimeter = _____
   area = _____

3. h = 3.6 km
   b = 4.8 km
   c = 6 km
   perimeter = _____
   area = _____

4. h = 12 dm
   b = 12.6 dm
   c = 17.4 dm
   perimeter = _____
   area = _____

5.* h = 3.9 m
   b = 520 cm
   c = 6,500 mm
   perimeter = _____
   area = _____

Basic Computation Series 2000: Working with Perimeter and Area
SECTION 3 Perimeter and Area of Triangles, Parallelograms, and Trapezoids

NAME DATE

Perimeter and Area of Right Triangles – English Units

Find the perimeter and area of the right triangle shown given each set of dimensions. In problems marked *, be sure to convert the dimensions to the same units.

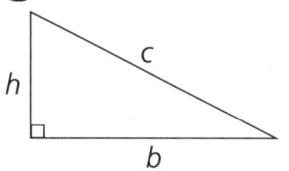

1. h = 16 ft
   b = 30 ft
   c = 34 ft
   perimeter = __80 ft__
   area = __240 ft²__

2. h = 18 in.
   b = 80 in.
   c = 82 in.
   perimeter = _____
   area = _____

3. h = 36 yd
   b = 77 yd
   c = 85 yd
   perimeter = _____
   area = _____

4. h = 65 ft
   b = 72 ft
   c = 97 ft
   perimeter = _____
   area = _____

5.* h = 13 in.
   b = 7 ft
   c = 85 in.
   perimeter = _____
   area = _____

Basic Computation Series 2000: Working with Perimeter and Area
SECTION 3 Perimeter and Area of Triangles, Parallelograms, and Trapezoids

NAME _____ DATE _____

Perimeter and Area of Right Triangles – Metric Units

Find the perimeter and area of the right triangle shown given each set of dimensions. In problems marked *, be sure to convert the dimensions to the same units.

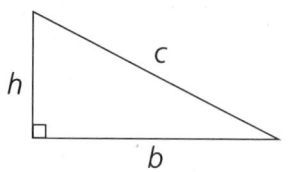

1. h = 21 cm
   b = 28 cm
   c = 35 cm
   perimeter = __84 cm__
   area = __294 cm²__

2. h = 14 mm
   b = 48 mm
   c = 50 mm
   perimeter = _____
   area = _____

3. h = 3.3 cm
   b = 5.6 cm
   c = 6.5 cm
   perimeter = _____
   area = _____

4. h = 0.11 dm
   b = 0.60 dm
   c = 0.61 dm
   perimeter = _____
   area = _____

5.* h = 3.9 m
   b = 0.008 km
   c = 890 cm
   perimeter = _____
   area = _____

Basic Computation Series 2000: Working with Perimeter and Area
SECTION 3 Perimeter and Area of Triangles, Parallelograms, and Trapezoids

Area of Triangles

For each triangle, find the number of units in the base and height, and the number of square units in the area.

1. base = __9__
   height = __4__
   area = __18__

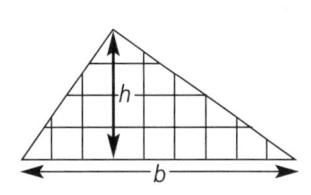

2. base = _____
   height = _____
   area = _____

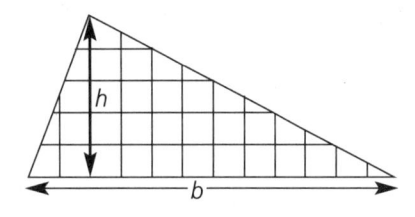

3. base = _____
   height = _____
   area = _____

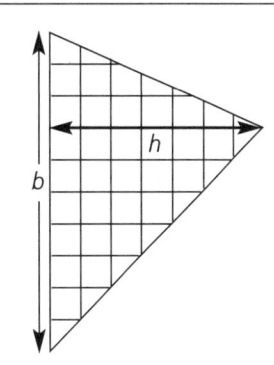

4. base = _____
   height = _____
   area = _____

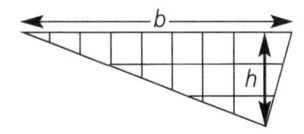

5. base = _____
   height = _____
   area = _____

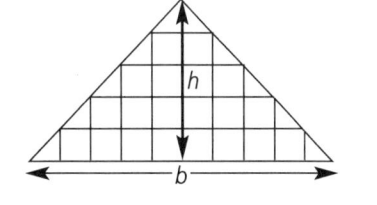

NAME _____ DATE _____

Drawing Triangles with Given Dimensions or Area

For each problem, draw three different-shaped triangles, each having the given dimensions. Make one triangle in each problem a right triangle. Then find the area of the triangles.

1. base = 6 units
   height = 5 units
   area = _____

2. base = 9 units
   height = 4 units
   area = _____

3. base = 12 units
   height = 3 units
   area = _____

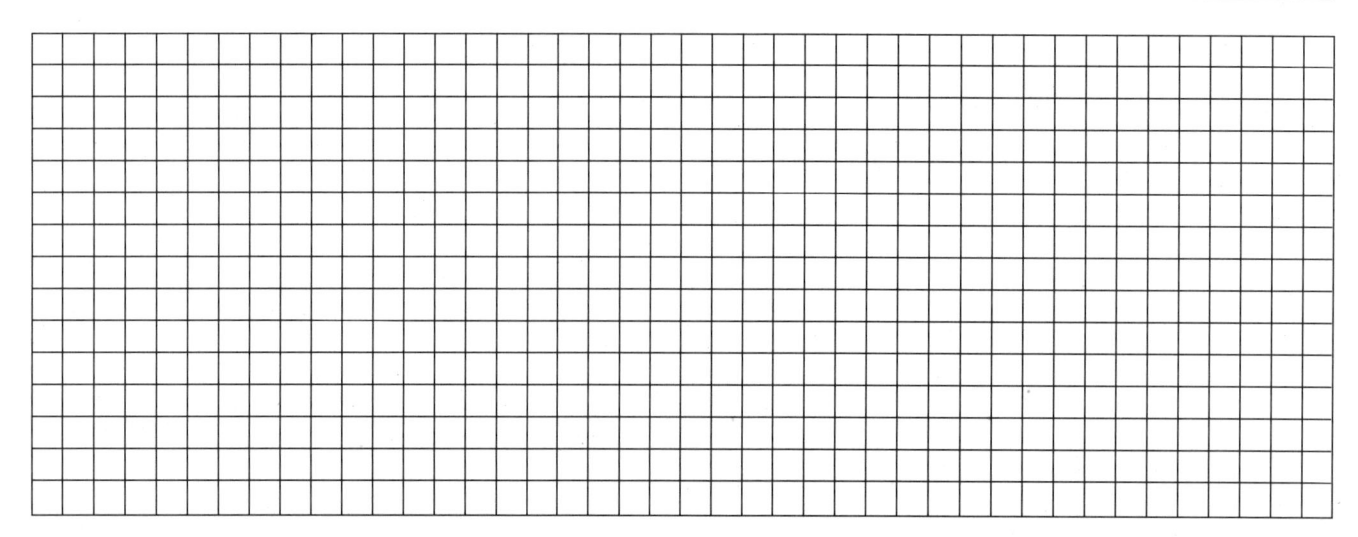

For each problem, draw three different-shaped triangles, each having the given area. Label each triangle with the number of units in the base and the height.

4. area = 14 units²

5. area = 16 units²

6. area = 10 units²

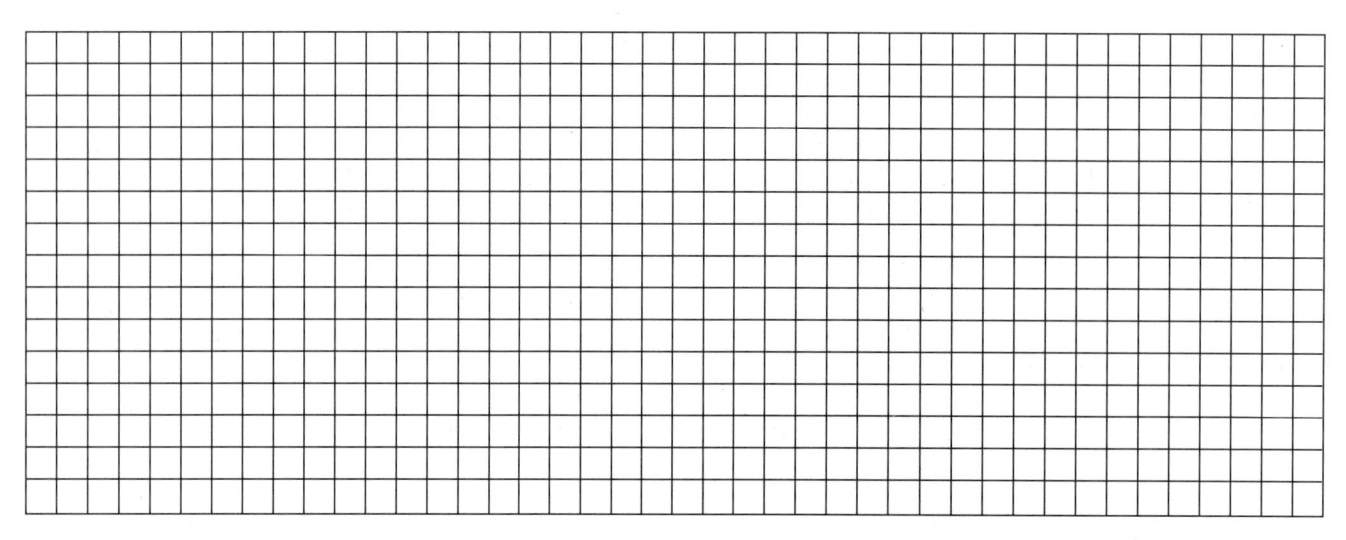

Basic Computation Series 2000: Working with Perimeter and Area

SECTION 3 Perimeter and Area of Triangles, Parallelograms, and Trapezoids

NAME DATE

Area of Triangles

For each triangle, find the number of units in the base and height, and the number of square units in the area.

1. base = __11__
   height = __5__
   area = __27½__

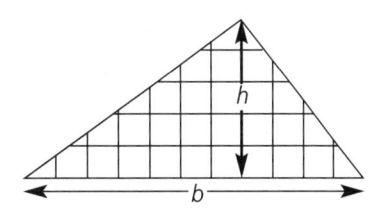

2. base = _____
   height = _____
   area = _____

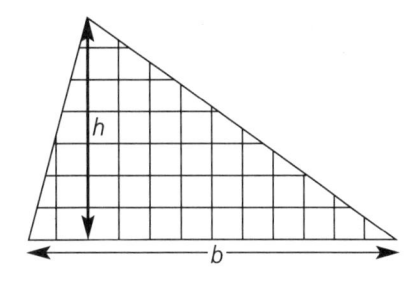

3. base = _____
   height = _____
   area = _____

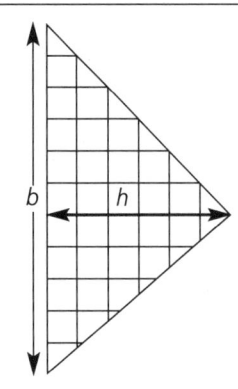

4. base = _____
   height = _____
   area = _____

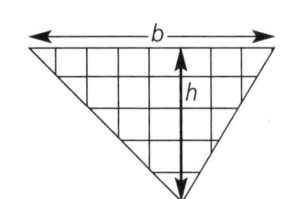

5. base = _____
   height = _____
   area = _____

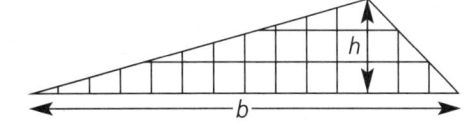

Basic Computation Series 2000: Working with Perimeter and Area
SECTION 3 Perimeter and Area of Triangles, Parallelograms, and Trapezoids

NAME _____ DATE _____

Drawing Triangles with Given Dimensions or Area

For each problem, draw three different-shaped triangles, each having the given dimensions. Make one triangle in each problem a right triangle. Then find the area of the triangles.

1. base = 7 units
   height = 4 units
   area = _____

2. base = 10 units
   height = 9 units
   area = _____

3. base = 12 units
   height = 12 units
   area = _____

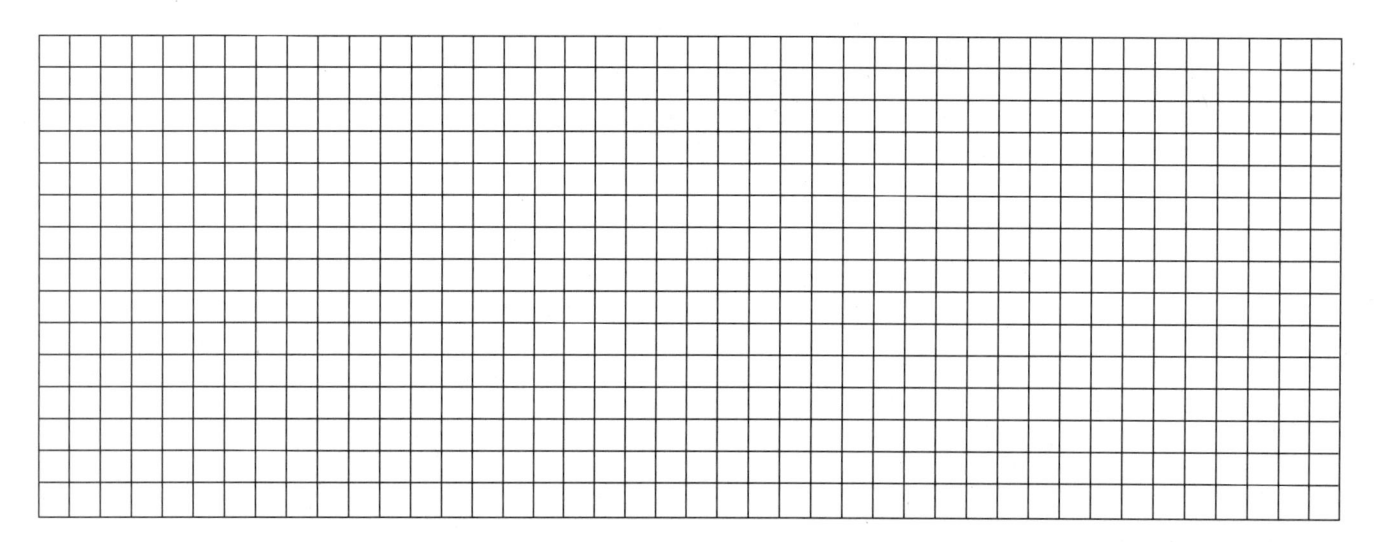

For each problem, draw three different-shaped triangles, each having the given area. Label each triangle with the number of units in the base and the height.

4. area = 20 units²

5. area = 18 units²

6. area = 12 units²

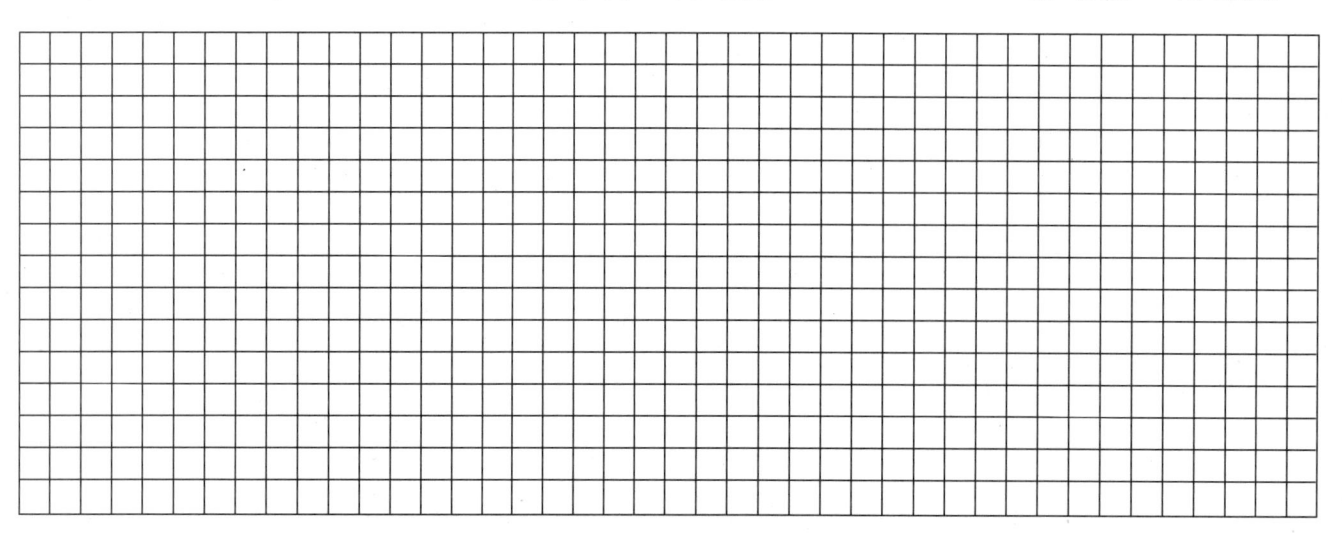

Basic Computation Series 2000: Working with Perimeter and Area

SECTION 3 Perimeter and Area of Triangles, Parallelograms, and Trapezoids

NAME

DATE

Area of Triangles

For each triangle, find the number of units in the base and height, and the number of square units in the area.

1. base = __13__

   height = __5__

   area = __$32\frac{1}{2}$__

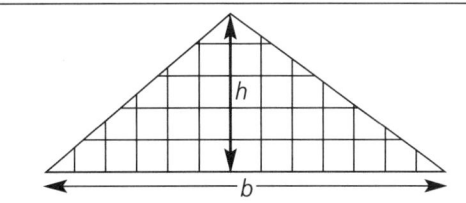

2. base = _____

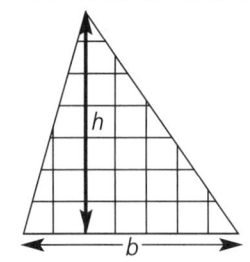

   height = _____

   area = _____

3. base = _____

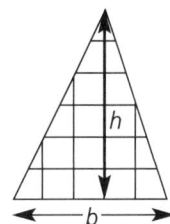

   height = _____

   area = _____

4. base = _____

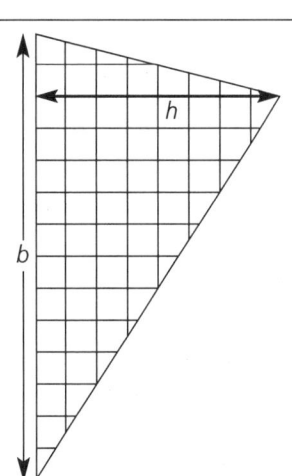

   height = _____

   area = _____

5. base = _____

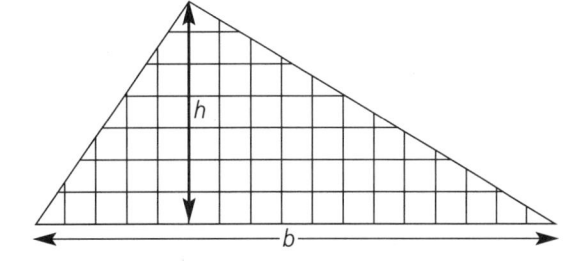

   height = _____

   area = _____

Basic Computation Series 2000: Working with Perimeter and Area
SECTION 3 Perimeter and Area of Triangles, Parallelograms, and Trapezoids

NAME _____ DATE _____

Drawing Triangles with Given Dimensions or Area

For each problem, draw three different-shaped triangles, each having the given dimensions. Make one triangle in each problem a right triangle. Then find the area of the triangles.

1. base = 8 units

height = 4 units

area = _____

2. base = 10 units

height = 5 units

area = _____

3. base = 7 units

height = 6 units

area = _____

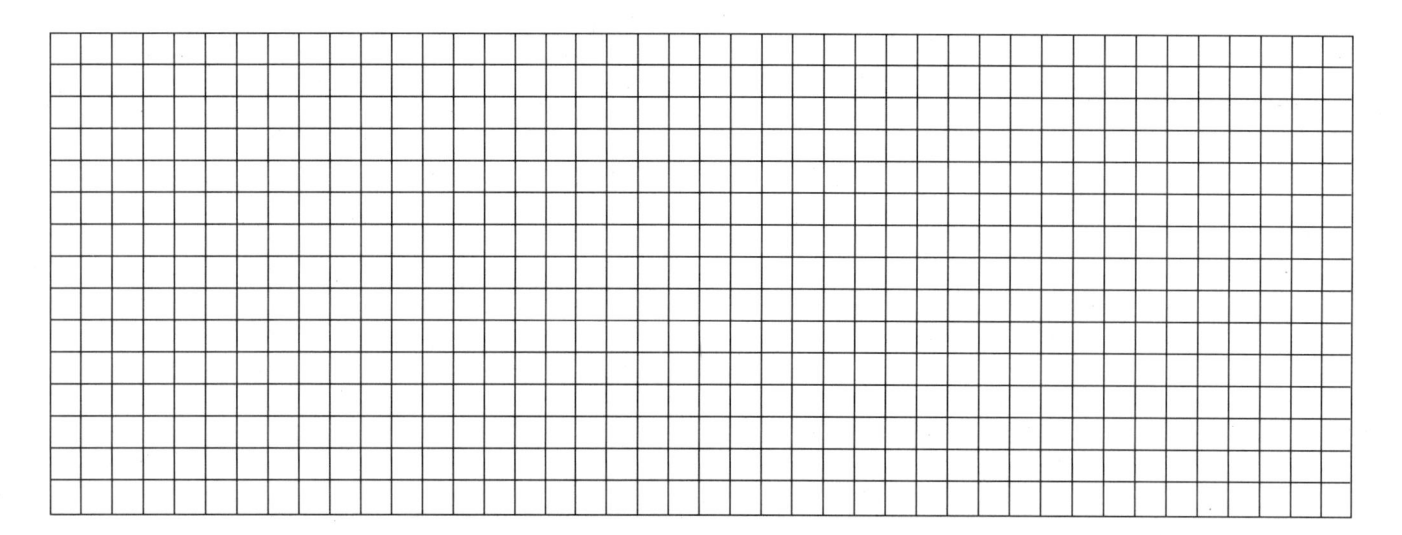

For each problem, draw three different-shaped triangles, each having the given area. Label each triangle with the number of units in the base and the height.

4. area = 15 units^2

5. area = 26 units^2

6. area = 18 units^2

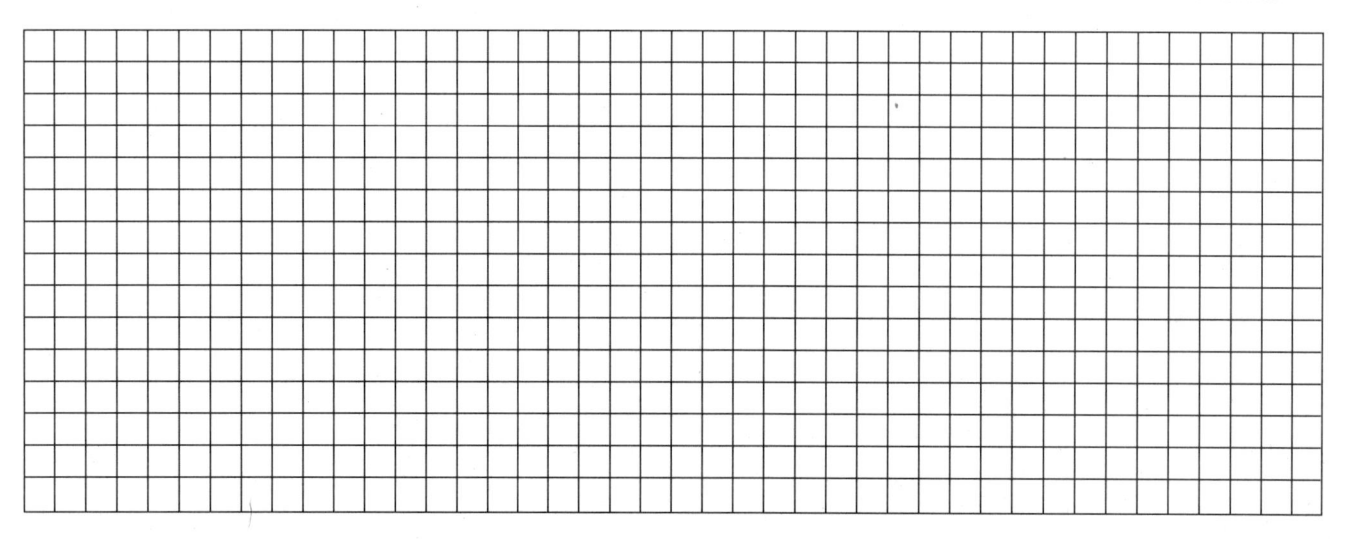

76

Basic Computation Series 2000: Working with Perimeter and Area
SECTION 3 Perimeter and Area of Triangles, Parallelograms, and Trapezoids

Copyright © Dale Seymour Publications®

NAME   DATE

Area of Triangles

For each triangle, find the number of units in the base and height, and the number of square units in the area.

1. base = __13__

height = __4__

area = __26__

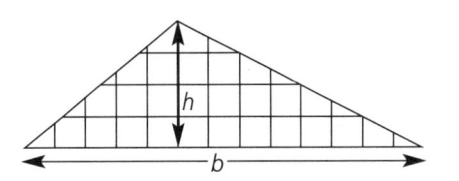

2. base = _____

height = _____

area = _____

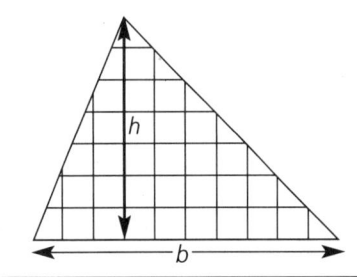

3. base = _____

height = _____

area = _____

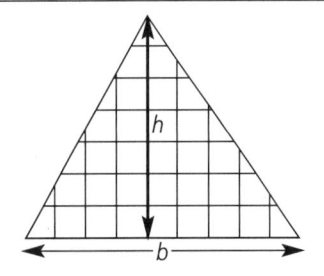

4. base = _____

height = _____

area = _____

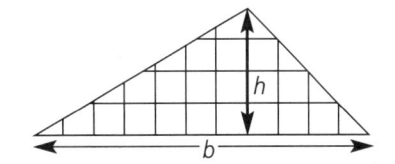

5. base = _____

height = _____

area = _____

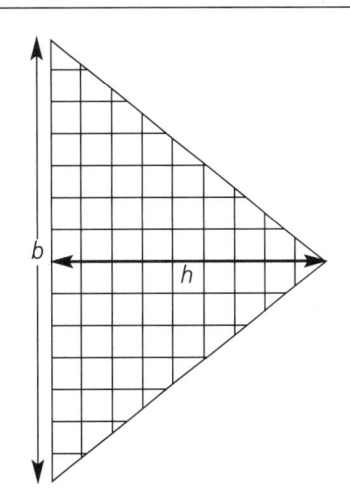

Basic Computation Series 2000: Working with Perimeter and Area
SECTION 3 Perimeter and Area of Triangles, Parallelograms, and Trapezoids

NAME
DATE

Drawing Triangles with Given Dimensions or Area

For each problem, draw three different-shaped triangles, each having the given dimensions. Make one triangle in each problem a right triangle. Then find the area of the triangles.

1. base = 9 units

height = 12 units

area = _____

2. base = 13 units

height = 8 units

area = _____

3. base = 7 units

height = 14 units

area = _____

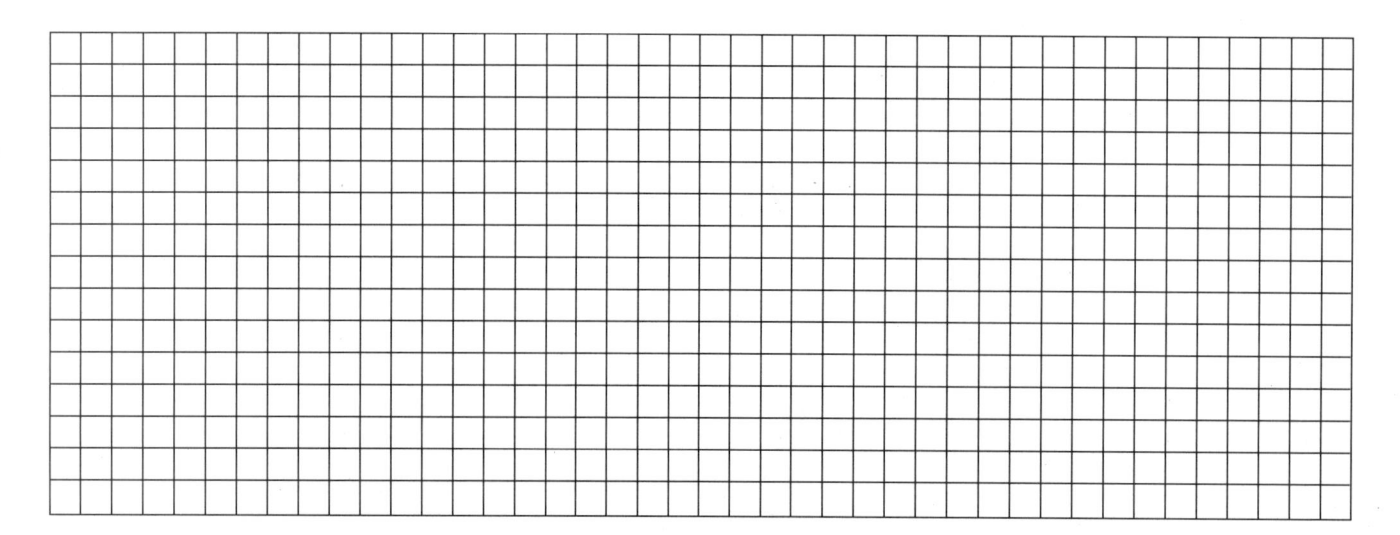

For each problem, draw three different-shaped triangles, each having the given area. Label each triangle with the number of units in the base and the height.

4. area = 22 units^2

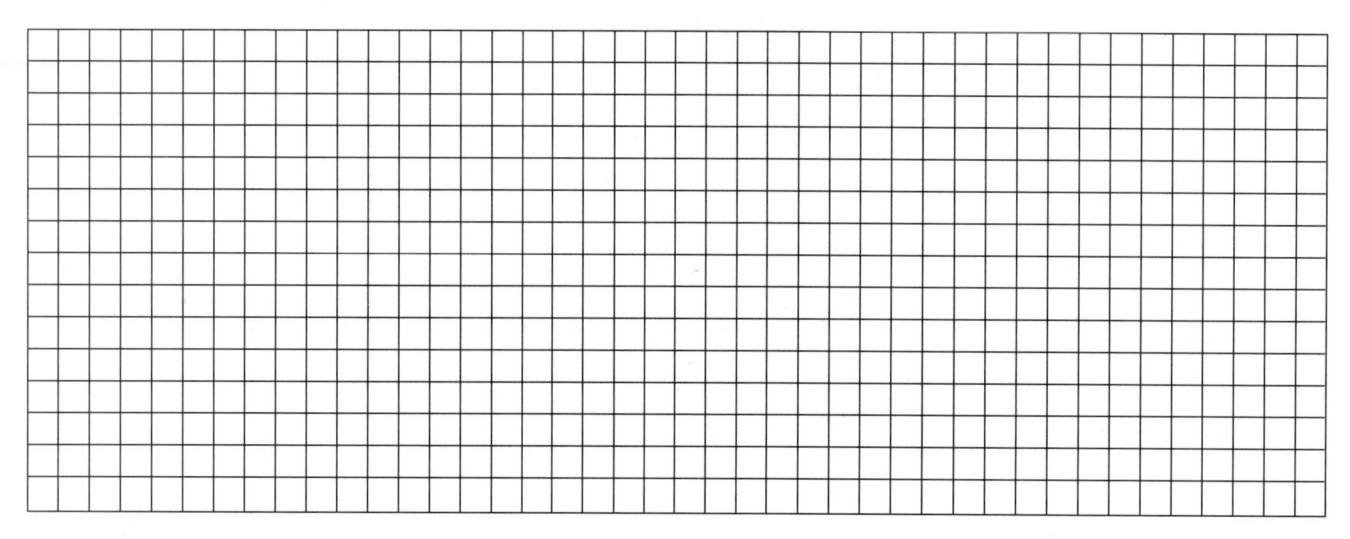

5. area = 14 units^2

6. area = 9 units^2

78

Basic Computation Series 2000: Working with Perimeter and Area

SECTION 3 Perimeter and Area of Triangles, Parallelograms, and Trapezoids

NAME _____   DATE _____

Area of Triangles

For each triangle, find the number of units in the base and height, and the number of square units in the area.

1. base = __13__
   height = __4__
   area = __26__

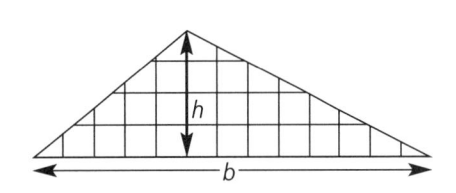

2. base = _____
   height = _____
   area = _____

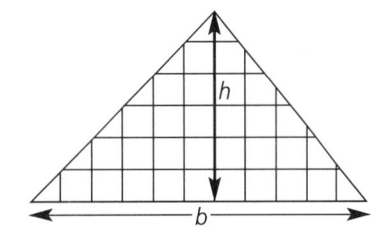

3. base = _____
   height = _____
   area = _____

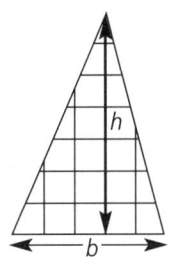

4. base = _____
   height = _____
   area = _____

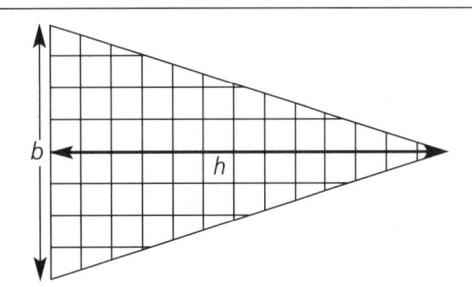

5. base = _____
   height = _____
   area = _____

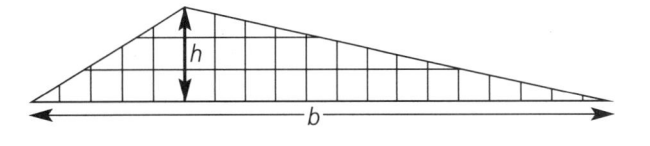

Basic Computation Series 2000: Working with Perimeter and Area
SECTION 3 Perimeter and Area of Triangles, Parallelograms, and Trapezoids

Drawing Triangles with Given Dimensions or Area

For each problem, draw three different-shaped triangles, each having the given dimensions. Make one triangle in each problem a right triangle. Then find the area of the triangles.

1. base = 9 units
   height = 4 units
   area = _____

2. base = 12 units
   height = 5 units
   area = _____

3. base = 11 units
   height = 8 units
   area = _____

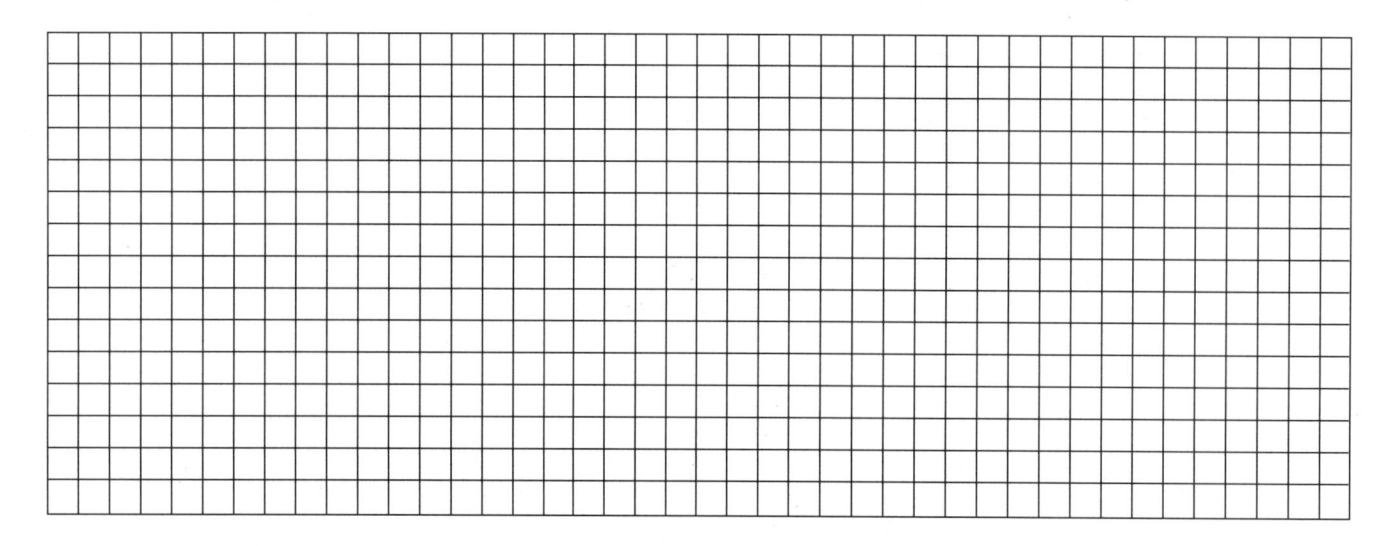

For each problem, draw three different-shaped triangles, each having the given area. Label each triangle with the number of units in the base and the height.

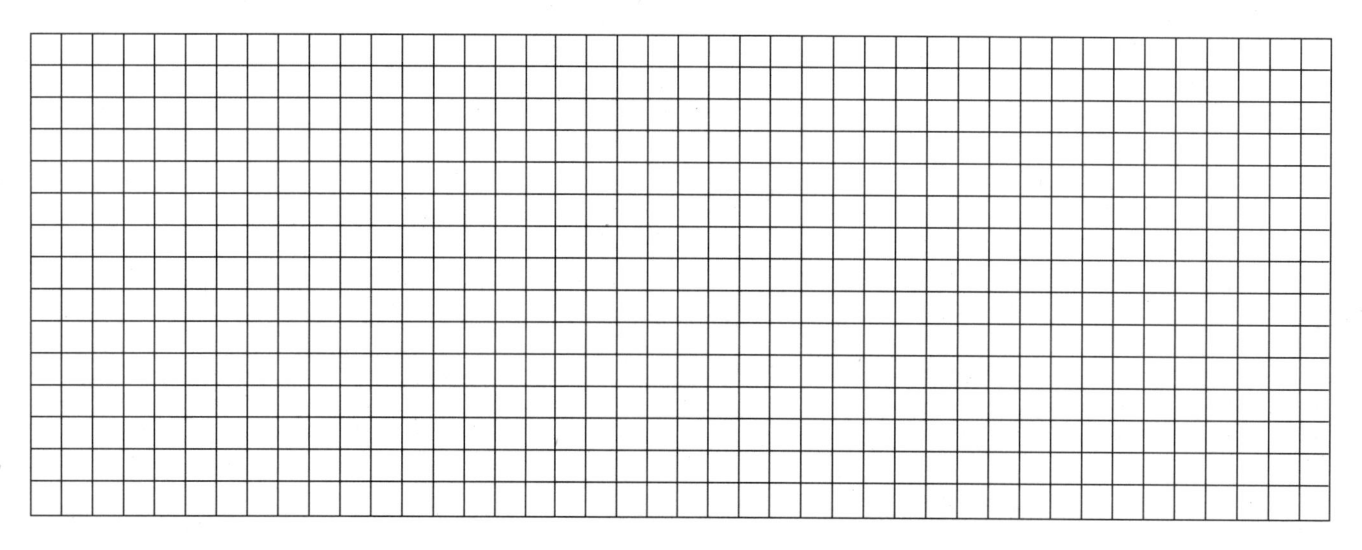

4. area = 25 units²

5. area = 15 units²

6. area = 28 units²

Basic Computation Series 2000: Working with Perimeter and Area

SECTION 3 Perimeter and Area of Triangles, Parallelograms, and Trapezoids

Area and Perimeter of Triangles and Parallelograms

Find the number of square units in the area and the number of units in the perimeter of the triangle shown given each set of dimensions.

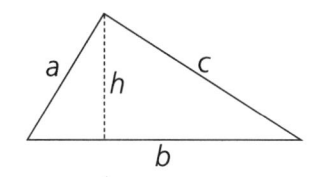

	a	b	c	h	area	perimeter
1.	40	39	25	24	468	104
2.	20	21	13	12		
3.	25	36	29	20		

Find the number of square units in the area and the number of units in the perimeter of the parallelogram shown given each set of dimensions.

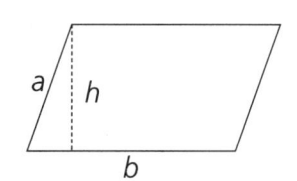

	a	b	h	area	perimeter
4.	15	20	9		
5.	18	31	12		
6.	30	27	18		

Basic Computation Series 2000: Working with Perimeter and Area
SECTION 3 Perimeter and Area of Triangles, Parallelograms, and Trapezoids

NAME   DATE

Area and Perimeter of Trapezoids

Find the number of square units in the area and the number of units in the perimeter of the trapezoid shown given each set of dimensions.

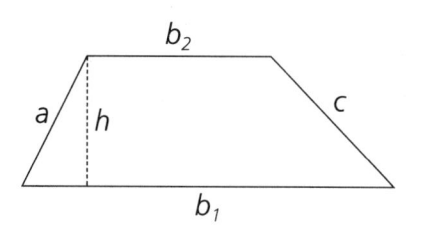

1. $a = 25$ area = __680__
   $b_1 = 53$ perimeter = __119__
   $b_2 = 17$
   $c = 29$ $A = \frac{1}{2} h (b_1 + b_2)$
   $h = 20$ $A = \frac{1}{2} (20)(53 + 17)$
                $A = (10)(70)$
                $A = 700$

   $P = a + b_1 + b_2 + c$
   $P = 25 + 53 + 17 + 29$
   $P = 124$

2. $a = 15$ area = _____
   $b_1 = 28$ perimeter = _____
   $b_2 = 14$
   $c = 13$
   $h = 12$

3. $a = 85$ area = _____
   $b_1 = 143$ perimeter = _____
   $b_2 = 51$
   $c = 39$
   $h = 36$

4. $a = 53$ area = _____
   $b_1 = 96$ perimeter = _____
   $b_2 = 30$
   $c = 35$
   $h = 28$

Basic Computation Series 2000: Working with Perimeter and Area
SECTION 3 Perimeter and Area of Triangles, Parallelograms, and Trapezoids

Area and Perimeter of Triangles and Parallelograms

Find the number of square units in the area and the number of units in the perimeter of the triangle shown given each set of dimensions.

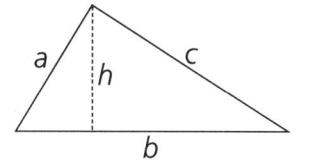

	a	b	c	h	area	perimeter
1.	100	91	61	60	2,730	252
2.	123	156	45	27		
3.	13	40	37	12		

Find the number of square units in the area and the number of units in the perimeter of the parallelogram shown given each set of dimensions.

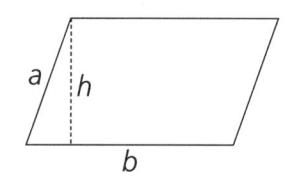

	a	b	h	area	perimeter
4.	20	35	16		
5.	17	27	14		
6.	34	32	19		

Basic Computation Series 2000: Working with Perimeter and Area
SECTION 3 Perimeter and Area of Triangles, Parallelograms, and Trapezoids

Area and Perimeter of Trapezoids

Find the number of square units in the area and the number of units in the perimeter of the trapezoid shown given each set of dimensions.

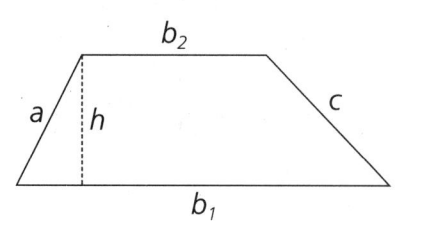

1. $a = 25$ area = __680__
$b_1 = 53$ perimeter = __119__
$b_2 = 17$
$c = 29$ $A = \frac{1}{2} h (b_1 + b_2)$
$h = 20$ $A = \frac{1}{2} (20)(53 + 17)$
             $A = (10)(70)$
             $A = 700$

$P = a + b_1 + b_2 + c$
$P = 25 + 53 + 17 + 29$
$P = 124$

2. $a = 41$ area = _____
$b_1 = 111$ perimeter = _____
$b_2 = 72$
$c = 50$
$h = 40$

3. $a = 89$ area = _____
$b_1 = 170$ perimeter = _____
$b_2 = 38$
$c = 65$
$h = 39$

4. $a = 104$ area = _____
$b_1 = 131$ perimeter = _____
$b_2 = 26$
$c = 41$
$h = 40$

Area and Perimeter of Triangles and Parallelograms

Find the number of square units in the area and the number of units in the perimeter of the triangle shown given each set of dimensions.

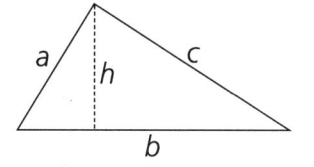

	a	b	c	h	area	perimeter
1.	25	28	17	15	210	70
2.	52	69	29	20		
3.	20	42	34	16		

Find the number of square units in the area and the number of units in the perimeter of the parallelogram shown given each set of dimensions.

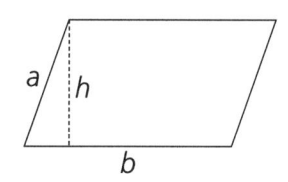

	a	b	h	area	perimeter
4.	15	16	7		
5.	24	28	16		
6.	26	31	21		

Basic Computation Series 2000: Working with Perimeter and Area
SECTION 3 Perimeter and Area of Triangles, Parallelograms, and Trapezoids

NAME _____ DATE _____

Area and Perimeter of Trapezoids

Find the number of square units in the area and the number of units in the perimeter of the trapezoid shown given each set of dimensions.

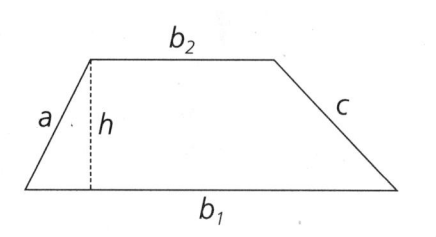

---

1. $a = 25$ area = __680__
  $b_1 = 53$ perimeter = __119__
  $b_2 = 17$
  $c = 29$ $A = \frac{1}{2} h (b_1 + b_2)$
  $h = 20$ $A = \frac{1}{2} (20)(53 + 17)$
         $A = (10)(70)$
         $A = 700$

  $P = a + b_1 + b_2 + c$
  $P = 25 + 53 + 17 + 29$
  $P = 124$

2. $a = 20$ area = _____
  $b_1 = 71$ perimeter = _____
  $b_2 = 20$
  $c = 37$
  $h = 12$

3. $a = 109$ area = _____
  $b_1 = 154$ perimeter = _____
  $b_2 = 31$
  $c = 68$
  $h = 60$

4. $a = 65$ area = _____
  $b_1 = 128$ perimeter = _____
  $b_2 = 53$
  $c = 20$
  $h = 16$

Basic Computation Series 2000: Working with Perimeter and Area
SECTION 3 Perimeter and Area of Triangles, Parallelograms, and Trapezoids

Area and Perimeter of Triangles and Parallelograms

Find the number of square units in the area and the number of units in the perimeter of the triangle shown given each set of dimensions.

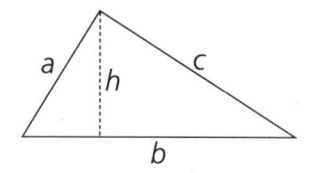

	a	b	c	h	area	perimeter
1.	20	51	37	12	306	108
2.	80	84	52	48		
3.	30	25	25	24		

Find the number of square units in the area and the number of units in the perimeter of the parallelogram shown given each set of dimensions.

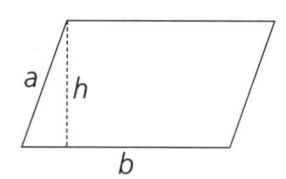

	a	b	h	area	perimeter
4.	18	16	15		
5.	21	29	18		
6.	28	31	24		

Basic Computation Series 2000: Working with Perimeter and Area
SECTION 3 Perimeter and Area of Triangles, Parallelograms, and Trapezoids

NAME _____   DATE _____

Area and Perimeter of Trapezoids

Find the number of square units in the area and the number of units in the perimeter of the trapezoid shown given each set of dimensions.

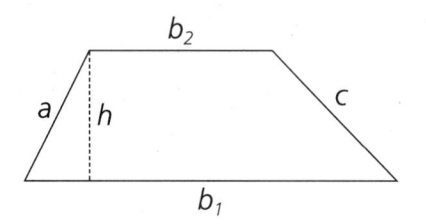

1. $a = 25$ area = __680__
$b_1 = 53$ perimeter = __119__
$b_2 = 17$
$c = 29$ $A = \frac{1}{2} h (b_1 + b_2)$
$h = 20$ $A = \frac{1}{2} (20)(53 + 17)$
$A = (10)(70)$
$A = 700$

$P = a + b_1 + b_2 + c$
$P = 25 + 53 + 17 + 29$
$P = 124$

2. $a = 25$ area = _____
$b_1 = 51$ perimeter = _____
$b_2 = 15$
$c = 29$
$h = 20$

3. $a = 61$ area = _____
$b_1 = 54$ perimeter = _____
$b_2 = 18$
$c = 65$
$h = 60$

4. $a = 41$ area = _____
$b_1 = 102$ perimeter = _____
$b_2 = 56$
$c = 15$
$h = 9$

Area and Perimeter of Triangles and Parallelograms

Find the number of square units in the area and the number of units in the perimeter of the triangle shown given each set of dimensions.

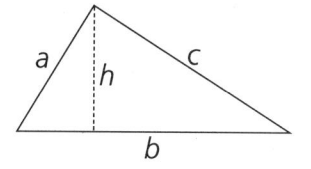

	a	b	c	h	area	perimeter
1.	68	43	61	60	1,290	172
2.	75	92	29	21		
3.	15	44	37	12		

Find the number of square units in the area and the number of units in the perimeter of the parallelogram shown given each set of dimensions.

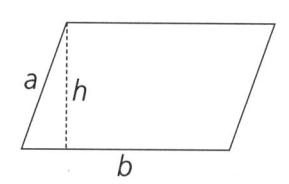

	a	b	h	area	perimeter
4.	21	17	19		
5.	25	35	17		
6.	36	42	31		

Basic Computation Series 2000: Working with Perimeter and Area
SECTION 3 Perimeter and Area of Triangles, Parallelograms, and Trapezoids

Area and Perimeter of Trapezoids

Find the number of square units in the area and the number of units in the perimeter of the trapezoid shown given each set of dimensions.

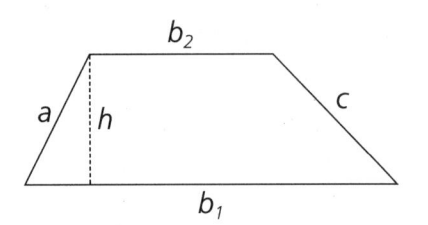

1. $a = 25$ area = __680__
   $b_1 = 53$ perimeter = __119__
   $b_2 = 17$
   $c = 29$ $A = \frac{1}{2} h (b_1 + b_2)$
   $h = 20$ $A = \frac{1}{2} (20)(53 + 17)$
              $A = (10)(70)$
              $A = 700$

   $P = a + b_1 + b_2 + c$
   $P = 25 + 53 + 17 + 29$
   $P = 124$

2. $a = 78$ area = _____
   $b_1 = 146$ perimeter = _____
   $b_2 = 34$
   $c = 50$
   $h = 30$

3. $a = 58$ area = _____
   $b_1 = 107$ perimeter = _____
   $b_2 = 55$
   $c = 150$
   $h = 42$

4. $a = 58$ area = _____
   $b_1 = 77$ perimeter = _____
   $b_2 = 26$
   $c = 41$
   $h = 40$

Answers to Exercises

PAGE 4
1. 10, 10, 40, 100 **2.** 10, 6, 32, 60 **3.** 13, 6, 38, 78 **4.** 13, 4, 34, 52 **5.** 6, 5, 22, 30

PAGE 5
1. 9, 3, 24, 27 **2.** 8, 4, 24, 32 **3.** 7, 2, 18, 14 **4.** 15, 5, 40, 75 **5.** 17, 2, 38, 34

PAGE 6
1. 15, 12, 54, 180 **2.** 3, 11, 28, 33 **3.** 9, 1, 20, 9 **4.** 3, 6, 18, 18 **5.** 14, 6, 40, 84

PAGE 7
1. 6, 11, 34, 66 **2.** 13, 11, 48, 143 **3.** 11, 5, 32, 55 **4.** 8, 7, 30, 56 **5.** 22, 5, 54, 110

PAGE 8
1. 12, 6, 36, 72 **2.** 5, 10, 30, 50 **3.** 27, 3, 60, 81 **4.** 5, 11, 32, 55 **5.** 4, 9, 26, 36

PAGE 9
1. 6, 15, 42, 90 **2.** 10, 17, 54, 170 **3.** 9, 12, 42, 108 **4.** 2, 11, 26, 22 **5.** 12, 5, 34, 60

PAGE 10
1. 11, 16, 54, 176 **2.** 7, 11, 36, 77 **3.** 8, 5, 26, 40 **4.** 8, 6, 28, 48 **5.** 18, 2, 40, 36

PAGE 11
1. 7, 14, 42, 98 **2.** 1, 8, 18, 8 **3.** 5, 6, 22, 30 **4.** 17, 5, 44, 85 **5.** 25, 6, 62, 150

PAGE 12
1. 11, 10, 42, 110 **2.** 10, 8, 36, 80 **3.** 14, 16, 60, 224 **4.** 6, 12, 36, 72 **5.** 21, 2, 46, 42

PAGE 13
1. 12, 12, 48, 144 **2.** 14, 1, 30, 14 **3.** 10, 4, 28, 40 **4.** 7, 6, 26, 42 **5.** 16, 4, 40, 64

PAGE 14
(Note: Other answers possible.) **1.** 12, 1, 26; 6, 2, 16; 4, 3, 14 **2.** 20, 1, 42; 10, 2, 24; 5, 4, 18 **3.** 24, 1, 50; 12, 2, 28; 8, 3, 22 **4.** 18, 1, 38; 9, 2, 22; 6, 3, 18 **5.** 30, 1, 62; 15, 2, 34; 10, 3, 26 **6.** 10, 5, 50; 9, 6, 54; 8, 7, 56 **7.** 18, 1, 18; 17, 2, 34; 16, 3, 48 **8.** 13, 1, 13; 12, 2, 24; 11, 3, 33 **9.** 10, 1, 10; 9, 2, 18; 8, 3, 24 **10.** 12, 1, 12; 11, 2, 22; 10, 3, 30

PAGE 15
1. 7, 4 **2.** 9, 4 **3.** 8, 5 **4.** 8, 7 **5.** 9, 5

PAGE 16
(Note: Other answers possible.) **1.** 15, 4, 38; 12, 5, 34; 10, 6, 32 **2.** 100, 1, 202; 20, 5, 50; 10, 10, 40 **3.** 32, 1, 66; 16, 2, 36; 8, 4, 24 **4.** 42, 1, 86; 14, 3, 34; 7, 6, 26 **5.** 50, 1, 102; 25, 2, 54; 10, 5, 30 **6.** 19, 1, 19; 18, 2, 36; 17, 3, 51 **7.** 27, 1, 27; 26, 2, 52; 25, 3, 75 **8.** 6, 1, 6; 5, 2, 10; 4, 3, 12 **9.** 15, 1, 15; 14, 2, 28; 13, 3, 39 **10.** 22, 1, 22; 21, 2, 42; 20, 3, 60

PAGE 17
1. 12, 3 **2.** 12, 2 **3.** 15, 3 **4.** 6, 5 **5.** 5, 4

PAGE 18
(Note: Other answers possible.) **1.** 28, 1, 58; 14, 2, 32; 7, 4, 22 **2.** 64, 1, 130; 32, 2, 68; 8, 8, 32 **3.** 52, 1, 106; 26, 2, 56; 13, 4, 34 **4.** 42, 1, 86; 21, 2, 46; 7, 6, 26 **5.** 75, 1, 152; 25, 3, 56; 15, 5, 40 **6.** 8, 1, 8; 7, 2, 14; 5, 4, 20 **7.** 7, 3, 21; 6, 4, 24; 5, 5, 25 **8.** 16, 1, 16; 15, 2, 30; 14, 3, 42 **9.** 23, 1, 23; 22, 2, 44; 21, 3, 63 **10.** 24, 1, 24; 20, 5, 100; 15, 10, 150

PAGE 19
1. 5, 5 **2.** 18, 5 **3.** 11, 4 **4.** 8, 3 **5.** 12, 5

PAGE 20
(Note: Other answers possible.) **1.** 36, 1, 74; 18, 2, 40; 9, 4, 26 **2.** 30, 1, 62; 15, 2, 34; 10, 3, 26 **3.** 40, 1, 82; 20, 2, 44; 8, 5, 26 **4.** 72, 1, 146; 36, 2, 76; 18, 4, 44 **5.** 54, 1, 110; 18, 3, 42; 9, 6, 30 **6.** 7, 1, 7; 6, 2, 12; 5, 3, 15 **7.** 11, 1, 11; 10, 2, 20; 9, 3, 27 **8.** 17, 1, 17; 16, 2, 32; 15, 3, 45 **9.** 13, 1, 13; 12, 2, 24; 11, 3, 33 **10.** 15, 1, 15; 14, 2, 28; 13, 3, 39

PAGE 21
1. 20, 3 **2.** 9, 9 **3.** 6, 6 **4.** 20, 4 **5.** 12, 7

PAGE 22
(Note: Other answers possible.) **1.** 20, 1, 42; 10, 2, 24; 5, 4, 18 **2.** 45, 1, 92; 15, 3, 36; 9, 5, 28 **3.** 32, 1, 66; 16, 2, 36; 8, 4, 24 **4.** 56, 1, 114; 14, 4, 36; 8, 7, 30 **5.** 18, 1, 38; 9, 2, 22; 6, 3, 18 **6.** 5, 1, 5; 4, 2, 8; 3, 3, 9 **7.** 8, 1, 8; 7, 2, 14; 6, 3, 18 **8.** 10, 1, 10; 9, 2, 18; 8, 3, 24 **9.** 20, 1, 20; 18, 3, 54; 15, 6, 80 **10.** 6, 1, 6; 5, 2, 10; 4, 3, 12

PAGE 23
1. 8, 5 **2.** 6, 4 **3.** 8, 8 **4.** 8, 7 **5.** 8, 2

PAGE 27
1. 72 ft, 288 ft^2 **2.** 90 yd, 350 yd^2 **3.** 168 in., 1,715 in.^{2} **4.** 70 yd, 216 yd^2 **5.** 41 ft, 102 ft^2 (Note: Other answers possible if different units are used.)

PAGE 28
1. 4.32 m, 0.494 m^2 **2.** 4.04 cm, 0.544 cm^2 **3.** 64.046 m, 0.736 m^2 **4.** 5.82 km, 1.025 km^2 **5.** 3.74 cm, 0.432 cm^2 (Note: Other answers possible if different units are used.)

PAGE 29
1. 106 in., 630 in.^{2} **2.** 78 ft, 374 ft^2 **3.** 32 ft, 64 ft^2 **4.** $34\frac{2}{3}$ ft, 75 ft^2 **5.** $26\frac{1}{2}$ ft, 42 ft^2 (Note: Other answers possible if different units are used.)

PAGE 30
1. 33 dm, 66.96 dm^2 **2.** 358 cm, 8,004 cm^2 **3.** 9.6 m, 4.32 m^2 **4.** 249 m, 305 m^2 **5.** 22.825 m, 0.1425 m^2 (Note: Other answers possible if different units are used.)

PAGE 31
1. 40 ft, 96 ft^2 **2.** 48 ft, 135 ft^2 **3.** $42\frac{1}{2}$ ft, 111 ft^2 **4.** $27\frac{1}{3}$ yd, 46 yd^2 **5.** 82 in., 408 in.^{2} (Note: Other answers possible if different units are used.)

Basic Computation Series 2000: Working with Perimeter and Area
ANSWERS TO EXERCISES

PAGE 32
1. 14 dm, 9.01 dm² **2.** 11 m, 5.16 m² **3.** 174.4 mm, 103.2 mm² **4.** 346 m, 3,450 m² **5.** 28,000.046 mm, 322 mm² (Note: Other answers possible if different units are used.)

PAGE 33
1. 62 in., 238 in.² **2.** 35 ft, 66 ft² **3.** 154 ft, 1,470 ft² **4.** 56 ft, 195 ft² **5.** $66\frac{1}{3}$ ft, 273 ft² (Note: Other answers possible if different units are used.)

PAGE 34
1. 35.8 dm, 80.04 dm² **2.** 14.2 m, 12.04 m² **3.** 22.8 cm, 24.65 cm² **4.** 16.66 m, 1.863 m² **5.** 1,346 cm, 14,950 cm² (Note: Other answers possible if different units are used.)

PAGE 35
1. 136 in., 1,075 in.² **2.** 338 ft, 7,008 ft² **3.** 56 yd, 171 yd² **4.** 69 ft, 182 ft² **5.** $148\frac{1}{2}$ ft, 932 ft² (Note: Other answers possible if different units are used.)

PAGE 36
1. 3.76 cm, 0.448 cm² **2.** 29 mm, 50.74 mm² **3.** 2,890 cm, 165,000 cm² **4.** 256 cm, 4,095 cm² **5.** 164.0086 m, 0.3526 m² (Note: Other answers possible if different units are used.)

PAGE 37
1. 76 ft, 240 ft² **2.** 88 yd, 384 yd² **3.** 176 in., 1,152 in.² **4.** 82 in., 378 in.² **5.** 154 ft, 930 ft² **6.** $21\frac{3}{10}$ mi, $27\frac{1}{5}$ mi² **7.** $21\frac{1}{6}$ ft, 28 ft² **8.** 26 in., 90 in. **9.** 18 ft, 94 ft **10.** 105 ft, 1,470 ft² **11.** 128 yd, 4,608 yd²

PAGE 38
1. 43 cm, 113.16 cm² **2.** 22.66 m, 29.3532 m² **3.** 5.7 m, 17.8 m **4.** 4.03 mm, 146.06 mm **5.** 2.6 cm, 9.1 cm² **6.** 9.3 m, 80.91 m² **7.** 4.14 cm, 100.28 cm

PAGE 39
1. 40 ft, 75 ft² **2.** 56 in., 192 in.² **3.** 120 yd, 800 yd² **4.** 76 ft, 345 ft² **5.** 98 in., 544 in.² **6.** $11\frac{1}{2}$ ft, $7\frac{1}{2}$ ft² **7.** $27\frac{2}{3}$ yd, $47\frac{1}{2}$ yd² **8.** 7 ft, 52 ft **9.** 12 in., 76 in. **10.** 35 yd, 840 yd² **11.** 32 ft, 1,824 ft²

PAGE 40
1. 310 cm, 5,976 cm² **2.** 186 mm, 2,052 mm² **3.** 37 m, 84.46 m² **4.** 18.2 dm, 19.38 dm² **5.** 2.6 m, 14.8 m **6.** 3.59 cm, 17.4 cm **7.** 5.4 m, 21.06 m²

PAGE 41
1. 32 yd, 48 yd² **2.** 120 ft, 675 ft² **3.** 118 ft, 864 ft² **4.** 178 yd, 1,908 yd² **5.** $26\frac{1}{6}$ ft, 35 ft² **6.** $24\frac{5}{6}$ ft, $37\frac{5}{8}$ ft² **7.** $29\frac{1}{6}$ yd, 49 yd² **8.** 18 in., 82 in. **9.** 27 in., 126 in. **10.** 31 ft, 1,457 ft² **11.** $5\frac{1}{2}$ ft, $30\frac{1}{4}$ ft²

PAGE 42
1. 100 cm, 544 cm² **2.** 220 cm, 2,881 cm² **3.** 230 m, 2,116 m² **4.** 12.24 mm, 6.336 mm² **5.** 61 cm, 306 cm **6.** 4.3 m, 19.8 m **7.** 36 mm, 1,548 mm²

PAGE 43
1. 82 ft, 364 ft² **2.** 148 ft, 928 ft² **3.** 212 in., 2,448 in.² **4.** 166 yd, 1,482 yd² **5.** $35\frac{2}{3}$ ft, 77 ft² **6.** $22\frac{5}{6}$ ft, $31\frac{1}{3}$ ft² **7.** $41\frac{1}{6}$ yd, $104\frac{5}{6}$ yd² **8.** 28 in., 142 in. **9.** 43 in., 220 in. **10.** 27 in., 378 in.² **11.** 5 ft, 75 ft²

PAGE 44
1. 40 m, 75 m² **2.** 72 cm, 288 cm² **3.** 79.8 cm, 107.3 cm² **4.** 73 cm, 248 cm **5.** 96 mm, 318 mm **6.** 34 cm, 2,618 cm² **7.** 26 mm, 988 mm²

PAGE 45
1. 120 ft, 576 ft² **2.** 112 in., 703 in.² **3.** 136 in., 1,131 in.² **4.** 216 ft, 2,432 ft² **5.** 278 yd, 1,750 yd² **6.** $15\frac{1}{6}$ ft, 12 ft² **7.** $15\frac{1}{6}$ ft, $14\frac{1}{6}$ ft² **8.** 22 yd, $25\frac{5}{9}$ yd² **9.** 13 in., 84 in. **10.** 24 ft, 220 ft **11.** 17 in., 100 in.

PAGE 46
1. 168 mm, 1,508 mm² **2.** 51.4 cm, 136.5 cm² **3.** 4.454 m, 1.2051 m² **4.** 27.84 mm, 45.752 mm² **5.** 34.5 cm, 253 cm **6.** 203 m, 14,007 m² **7.** 27 mm, 1,674 mm²

PAGE 51
1. 11, 4, 22 **2.** 12, 5, 30 **3.** 10, 7, 35 **4.** 8, 10, 40 **5.** 8, 7, 28 **6.** 5, 6, 15 **7.** 8, 12, 48 **8.** 14, 7, 49

PAGE 52
(Note: Other answers possible.) **1.** 9, 8; 18, 4; 12, 6 **2.** 4, 12; 6, 8; 16, 3

PAGE 53
1. 11, 6, 33 **2.** 7, 4, 14 **3.** 10, 8, 40 **4.** 6, 8, 24 **5.** 17, 6, 51 **6.** 5, 6, 15 **7.** 14, 5, 35 **8.** 3, 5, $7\frac{1}{2}$

PAGE 54
(Note: Other answers possible.) **1.** 6, 10; 4, 15; 5, 12 **2.** 8, 10; 4, 20; 16, 5

PAGE 55
1. 13, 6, 39 **2.** 3, 8, 12 **3.** 10, 4, 20 **4.** 8, 8, 32 **5.** 6, 7, 21 **6.** 16, 3, 24 **7.** 12, 4, 24 **8.** 8, 6, 24

PAGE 56
(Note: Other answers possible.) **1.** 4, 6; 2, 12; 3, 8 **2.** 8, 2; 16, 1; 4, 4

PAGE 57
1. 13, 6, 39 **2.** 4, 6, 12 **3.** 9, 6, 27 **4.** 8, 6, 24 **5.** 11, 9, $49\frac{1}{2}$ **6.** 11, 4, 22 **7.** 8, 7, 28 **8.** 12, 4, 24

PAGE 58
(Note: Other answers possible.) **1.** 4, 5; 1, 20; 2, 10 **2.** 4, 10; 2, 20; 8, 5

PAGE 59
1. 11, 9, $49\frac{1}{2}$ **2.** 12, 3, 18 **3.** 9, 7, $31\frac{1}{2}$ **4.** 14, 10, 70 **5.** 9, 4, 18 **6.** 8, 9, 36 **7.** 15, 3, $22\frac{1}{2}$ **8.** 10, 4, 20

PAGE 60
(Note: Other answers possible.) **1.** 4, 9; 3, 12; 6, 6 **2.** 4, 8; 1, 32; 16, 2

PAGE 61
1. 210 in.², 70 in. **2.** 630 yd², 126 yd **3.** 1,320 ft², 176 ft **4.** 2,730 in.², 260 in. **5.** 840 yd², 140 yd

Basic Computation Series 2000: Working with Perimeter and Area
ANSWERS TO EXERCISES

PAGE 62
1. 924 km², 154 km **2.** 330 m², 132 m **3.** 5,670 cm², 378 cm
4. 1,560 cm², 208 cm **5.** 0.0546 m², 1.82 m (Note: Other answers possible if different units are used.)

PAGE 63
1. 990 ft², 220 ft **2.** 840 in.², 140 in. **3.** 150 yd², 60 yd
4. 1,386 in.², 198 in. **5.** 924 ft², 154 ft.

PAGE 64
1. 7.26 cm², 13.2 cm **2.** 19.2 m², 24 m **3.** 29.4 dm², 28 dm
4. 68.04 m², 50.4 m **5.** 6,480 cm², 540 cm (Note: Other answers possible if different units are used.)

PAGE 65
1. 120 ft², 60 ft **2.** 486 ft², 108 ft **3.** 4,320 in.², 360 in.
4. $52\frac{1}{2}$ yd², 35 yd **5.** 1,620 yd², 270 yd (Note: Other answers possible if different units are used.)

PAGE 66
1. 120.96 cm², 67.2 cm **2.** 48.6 mm², 36 mm **3.** 0.5376 km², 4.48 km **4.** 72.6 dkm², 44 dkm **5.** 0.135 km², 1.8 km (Note: Other answers possible if different units are used.)

PAGE 67
1. 216 in.², 72 in. **2.** 384 ft², 96 ft **3.** 11,520 yd², 720 yd
4. 1,920 in.², 240 in. **5.** 336 ft², 112 ft (Note: Other answers possible if different units are used.)

PAGE 68
1. 19.44 m², 21.6 m **2.** 0.588 km², 4.2 km **3.** 8.64 km², 14.4 km
4. 75.6 dm², 42 dm **5.** 10.14 m², 15.6 m (Note: Other answers possible if different units are used.)

PAGE 69
1. 240 ft², 80 ft **2.** 720 in.², 180 in. **3.** 1,386 yd², 198 yd
4. 2,340 ft², 234 ft **5.** 546 in.², 182 in. (Note: Other answers possible if different units are used.)

PAGE 70
1. 294 cm², 84 cm **2.** 336 mm², 112 mm **3.** 9.24 cm², 15.4 cm
4. 0.033 dm², 1.32 dm **5.** 15.6 m², 20.8 m (Note: Other answers possible if different units are used.)

PAGE 71
1. 9, 4, 18 **2.** 12, 5, 30 **3.** 10, 7, 35 **4.** 9, 3, $13\frac{1}{2}$ **5.** 10, 5, 25

PAGE 72
1. 15 units² **2.** 18 units² **3.** 18 units² **4.** 4, 7; 14, 2; 28, 1 **5.** 4, 8; 16, 2; 32, 1 **6.** 5, 4; 10, 2; 20, 1 (Note: Other answers possible for #4–6.)

PAGE 73
1. 11, 5, $27\frac{1}{2}$ **2.** 12, 7, 42 **3.** 11, 6, 33 **4.** 8, 5, 20 **5.** 14, 3, 21

PAGE 74
1. 14 units² **2.** 45 units² **3.** 72 units² **4.** 8, 5; 10, 4; 20, 2 **5.** 9, 4; 6, 6; 12, 3 **6.** 3, 8; 6, 4; 12, 2 (Note: Other answers possible for #4–6.)

PAGE 75
1. 13, 5, $32\frac{1}{2}$ **2.** 7, 7, $24\frac{1}{2}$ **3.** 5, 6, 15 **4.** 14, 8, 56 **5.** 17, 7, $59\frac{1}{2}$

PAGE 76
1. 16 units² **2.** 25 units² **3.** 21 units² **4.** 6, 5; 10, 3; 15, 2 **5.** 4, 13; 26, 2; 52, 1 **6.** 6, 6; 9, 4; 12, 3 (Note: Other answers possible for #4–6.)

PAGE 77
1. 13, 4, 26 **2.** 10, 7, 35 **3.** 9, 7, $31\frac{1}{2}$ **4.** 11, 4, 22 **5.** 14, 9, 63

PAGE 78
1. 54 units² **2.** 52 units² **3.** 49 units² **4.** 4, 11; 22, 2; 44, 1 **5.** 4, 7; 14, 2; 28, 1 **6.** 3, 6; 9, 2; 18, 1 (Note: Other answers possible for #4–6.)

PAGE 79
1. 13, 4, 26 **2.** 11, 6, 33 **3.** 5, 7, $17\frac{1}{2}$ **4.** 8, 13, 52 **5.** 19, 3, $28\frac{1}{2}$

PAGE 80
1. 18 units² **2.** 30 units² **3.** 44 units² **4.** 10, 5; 25, 2; 50, 1 **5.** 6, 5; 10, 3; 15, 2 **6.** 7, 8; 14, 4; 28, 2 (Note: Other answers possible for #4–6.)

PAGE 81
1. 468, 104 **2.** 126, 54 **3.** 360, 90 **4.** 180, 70 **5.** 372, 98 **6.** 486, 114

PAGE 82
1. 700, 124 **2.** 252, 70 **3.** 3,492, 318 **4.** 1,764, 214

PAGE 83
1. 2,730, 252 **2.** 2,106, 324 **3.** 240, 90 **4.** 560, 110 **5.** 378, 88 **6.** 608, 132

PAGE 84
1. 700, 124 **2.** 3,660, 274 **3.** 4,056, 362 **4.** 3,140, 302

PAGE 85
1. 210, 70 **2.** 690, 150 **3.** 336, 96 **4.** 112, 62 **5.** 448, 104 **6.** 651, 114

PAGE 86
1. 700, 124 **2.** 546, 148 **3.** 5,550, 362 **4.** 1,448, 266

PAGE 87
1. 306, 108 **2.** 2,016, 216 **3.** 300, 80 **4.** 240, 68 **5.** 522, 100 **6.** 744, 118

PAGE 88
1. 700, 124 **2.** 660, 120 **3.** 2,160, 198 **4.** 711, 214

PAGE 89
1. 1,290, 172 **2.** 966, 196 **3.** 264, 96 **4.** 323, 76 **5.** 595, 120 **6.** 1,302, 156

PAGE 90
1. 700, 124 **2.** 2,700, 308 **3.** 3,402, 370 **4.** 2,060, 202

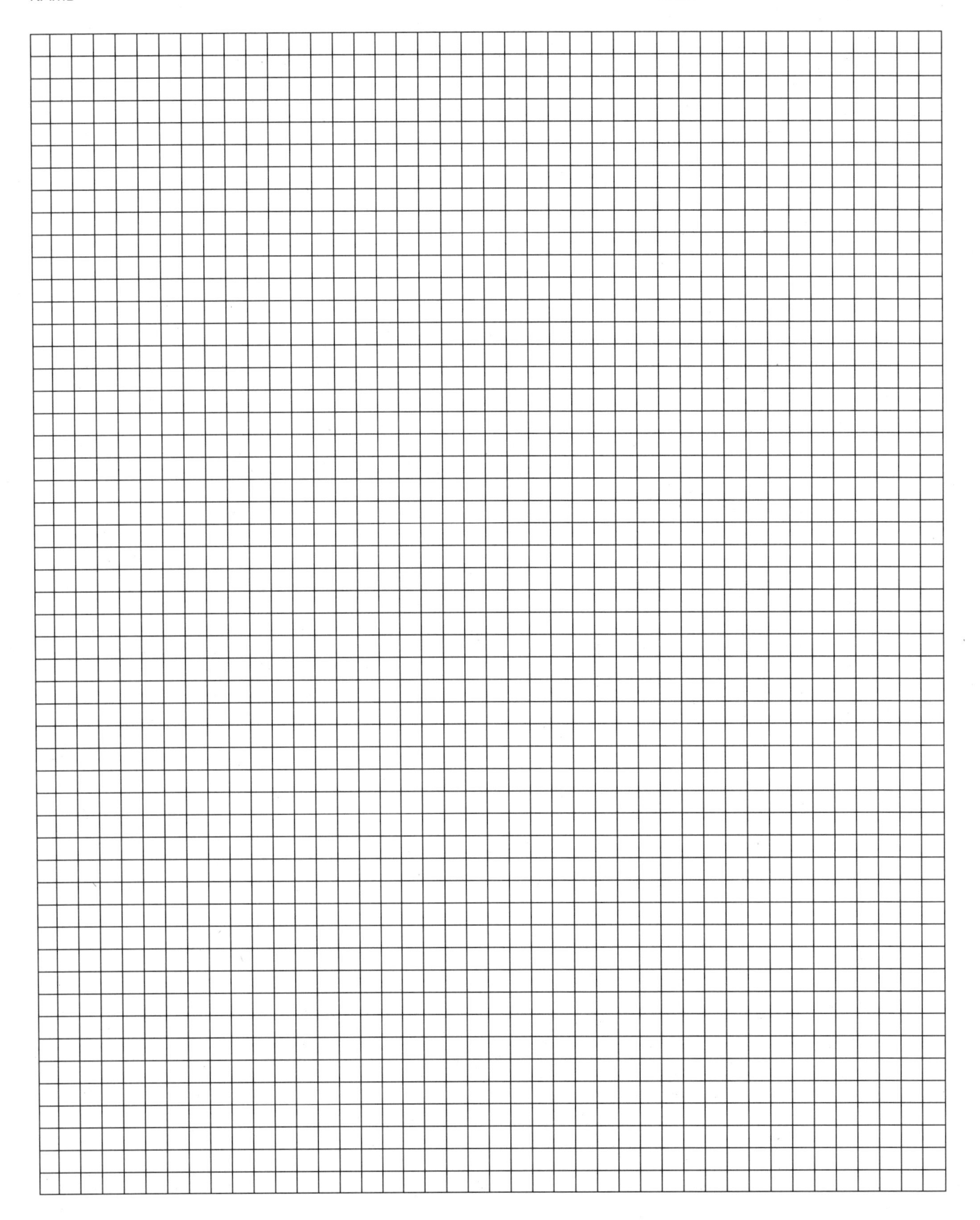